FLYING FAST AND LOW

Flying Fast and Low

The Story of Three Extraordinary Brothers

DAVID JAMES PARKER

First published in 2021 by Redshank Books

Redshank Books is an imprint of Libri Publishing.

Copyright © David James Parker

The right of David James Parker to be identified as the author of this work has been asserted in accordance with the Copyright, Designs and Patents Act, 1988.

ISBN 978-1-912969-22-7

Cover and book design by Carnegie Book Production

Printed in the UK by Severn

Libri Publishing
Brunel House
Volunteer Way
Faringdon
Oxfordshire
SN7 7YR

Tel: +44 (0)845 873 3837

www.libripublishing.co.uk

Disclaimer
Every effort has been taken to acknowledge copyright of images where possible. All other photographs and documents are from the author's collection.

Contents

Introduction

This is my second book on the Second World War with a similar theme to the first as it tells the story of brothers who served their country with pride and dedication. This is the extraordinary account of three brothers from the Muller-Rowland family: Eric, Stanley, and John Stuart, all of whom served in the Royal Air Force during the Second World War, two were killed in action and the third in 1950 while flying a development aircraft.

They were not professional airmen before the Second World War and their story is one of leadership, bravery, and devotion to duty. Eric initially signed up for the Honourable Artillery Company and transferred to the Royal Air Force, whereas his brothers, the twins, John Stuart, and Stanley enlisted in the Royal Air Force together.

Eric was lost while serving in North Africa taking part in raids on shipping in the Mediterranean flying Bristol Beaufighters. Stanley, a Squadron Leader and remarkable airman also flying Beaufighters, was lost in the North Sea after being hit by anti-aircraft fire.

John, the third brother, survived the war after flying operations in North Africa and Burma in Bristol Blenheims and Beaufighters. He became a test pilot in 1947. Passing out from the Empire Test Pilots School, he went on to succeed Lt/Cdr Eric (Winkle) Brown as commander of the Aero Flight at Farnborough. During his career prior to this he had flown a variety of different types of aircraft and as a test pilot a greater number of types were flown by him. At the forefront of jet aviation, he flew a number of the early jet aircraft as Britain strived to break the sound barrier.

It seems quite remarkable that this story has not been written previously. Stanley and John appear in numerous books, as part of the story but until now no-one has linked this information together. A simple search on the internet leads to several books and websites in which they get mentions. Even more so as John's obituary in 1950 was read by David Lean, which inspired him to make the film "Sound Barrier".

Talking to Mrs Wendy Walker, sister of the three brothers, gave me the inspiration for this project. It is rather ironic that I should have been talking to her on 27th September 2019. As her brother John was killed in the De Havilland 108 Swallow and this day happened to be the seventy third anniversary of Geoffrey De Havilland Jnr's death in the first Swallow.

The reader will see, as I did, that the brothers were remarkably good leaders and fearless in their fighting capability. It does make you wonder what they might have achieved had they lived.

As with my first book, my intention is again for this book to serve as a memorial to the brothers and to their crew members who lost their lives serving alongside them.

David James Parker

Kirdford 2021

Foreword

Air Commodore Graham Pitchfork MBE, FRAeS

During my years researching RAF history, particularly that of the Second World War, the name "Muller-Rowland" cropped up a few times. When I started researching for a book on the Beaufighter, their names became very familiar to me. It was soon clear that they had all made a significant contribution to the success of RAF low-level operations over land and sea. However, it was not until I read David Parker's book that I fully realised the scale of their respective operational and gallant service.

The three brothers flew in some of the most dangerous of all RAF operations. The losses amongst the Beaufighter crews were amongst the highest of any role. What they achieved in this demanding environment was truly remarkable, as their decorations make so clear.

As I read more of the text of this book, I began to draw parallels with some well-known and unique RAF families; the Atcherley brothers, the Beamish brothers, the remarkable Sowrey family. However, the greatest parallel was with the three MacRoberts brothers, who all died in the service of the RAF. Their mother, Lady MacRoberts, became famous for her resolve and determination to carry on the fight, not to mention her courage in the face of losing all her sons. I have always had the greatest admiration for her.

Now, I have been alerted to another remarkable mother. It is difficult, indeed impossible, to imagine the pain at the loss of all her sons and Daisy Muller-Rowland, like Lady MacRoberts, a bereaved mother who bore her burden with amazing courage and stoicism – a truly remarkable lady.

By publishing this book, David Parker has reminded us of this, until now, less well-known family, the Muller-Rowland boys, whose service and sacrifice stands alongside those other remarkable RAF families. I am pleased to have been able to record my respects to such gallant brothers.

Graham Pitchfork

Gloucestershire

February 2021

Acknowledgements

In the preparation of this book, I have several people to thank. First, I must thank Mrs Wendy Walker for telling me about her three brothers, which is the reason I got onto the book. Wendy's family, Claire, Tom, and Juliet who have offered support in the process and for them lending me the pilots' logbooks. Also, I must thank the family of Joy Mason, the eldest sister, Richard Mason, Jane Hoyle, David Mason and John Mason. To the family of Joan Powell, Carolyn Powell, Michael Powell, and Judy Clarke, for their additions and photographs.

The staff at National Archives have proved helpful on my various visits, pointing me in the direction of where to find things. To Steve Lane at Libri Publishing for showing the encouragement when I suggested what I wanted to write about. To Steve who runs the Petworth Book shop and stocked my first book and has encouraged me about this one.

An unusual one here, Margaret Kendall, (no relation to Alan) from the Manchester area, who, from a chance phone call did a little bit of research on my behalf and came up with something about Alan.

Thank you also to Air Commodore Graham Pitchfork for writing the foreword for the book.

Leslie Barton deserves a special thank you for allowing me to access her uncle, Alan Kendall's service records and for providing photographs. Leslie has also helped me with some of the editing.

I am also grateful to Alexandra, Stuart, and Jo Kent for allowing me to reproduce part of their father's book "One of the Few" and giving some information.

I will give a vote of thanks to Nick Harris of Pick Nick Photo Restoration and Design Services for the amazing job of colouring the photographs. nick@photorestoration.services

About the Author

David James Parker was born and brought up in Sussex. He has been interested in military history from an early age.

David started collecting items of militaria at ten years old when he found some medals in a bin. At secondary school David was inspired by his history teachers to learn more, which he carried on doing after leaving school. He has been giving talks about the First and Second World Wars for several years, using his extensive collections to illustrate these. David has written a companion book for his talks, "Fragments, A Collection in Words and Pictures, The First World War", with a book of "Fragments", covering his Second World War Home Front collection, in the process of being written. He also gives talks on the Royal Observer Corps and his life as a chimney sweep.

David served in the Royal Observer Corps for twelve years before joining the Army Cadet Force as an instructor for a further 29 years and still serving. He has had a few magazine articles published and one book to his credit, "Missing – the Wartime Account of Two Brothers". He has also had two chapters published in "As Memories Fade", a series of compilation books by his publishers.

He is a local chimney sweep, well known in his area. This leads him to meet a vast number of interesting people who are pleased to share their stories with him. He also gets to see many historic cottages and larger houses.

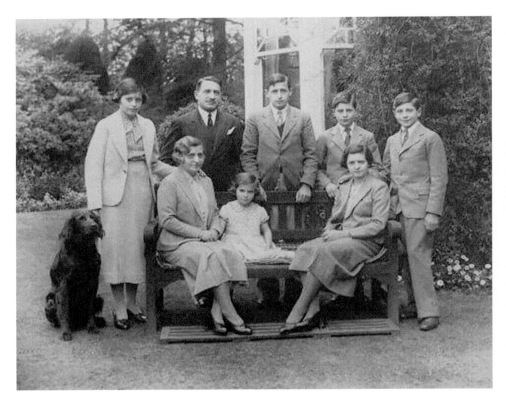

Family Portrait
Standing L-R Joan, John (Hans), Eric, Stuart, Stanley
Sitting L-R Daisy, Wendy and Joy

Dedication

I would like to dedicate this book to the family of Mrs Wendy Walker nee Muller-Rowland.

In memory of her three brothers, Eric, Stanley, and John, not forgetting the crews that died with Eric and Stanley.

Also, to Mrs Daisy Muller-Rowland who endured the loss of her three sons and continued to serve the community and inspire people.

From the Family (1)

When I heard that David Parker, a local historian with great interest in the Second World War, had met my Mum and was keen to write the story of the three Muller-Rowland Uncles that I never knew, it marked the beginning of investigating a family history that was rapidly receding into the distance.

My Mum, Wendy Walker, the youngest and only surviving member of her generation, adored her older brothers and Stuart in particular. Evacuated to Australia during the war on account of her age, her two sisters Joan and Joy played vital medical roles and remained in the UK.

After dedicated and meticulous research, David has unearthed a fascinating account of Eric, Stanley and Stuart who lived through extraordinary times and of a family who paid a high price for their country. Today it has brought the ten cousins together during 'Coronavirus-lockdown' as emails have flown back and forth, sharing what we know of family history. We are so grateful to David for his tremendous work in bringing to life the details of the three brothers' lives before these fade and are lost as important history for future generations.

Juliet Hindson, West Sussex, January 2021.

CHAPTER 1

The Muller-Rowland Family

Hans (also known as Jean as borne out in his application for naturalisation) Muller was born on 22nd July 1881 in Thayngen, Canton de Schaffhausen, Switzerland. Hans was the third of four children, Lina, Emile, and Emma. Their parents were Johannes, and his wife Verona (Veronica) Muller (nee Berath). Johannes was a farmer and insurance agent. Johannes was heavily involved in the local Lutheran Church and highly respected in the area. Despite this, Johannes was cold, austere, and repressive when it came to his family. Because of this the two boys left home as soon as they could. Emile fled to Portuguese East Africa (Mozambique). Hans left home at the age of sixteen to find himself a job. It appears that Hans was an intelligent lad and was introduced to the grain merchants, Louis Dreyfus, where he found employment, joining the company in 1900. One of the early postings for Hans was to

Hans (later John) Muller

Russia where he spent some years. Hans was deeply shocked by the level of poverty in Russia, which coming from his background must have been unknown. It was when Hans was posted to Hull that he met his future wife, Daisy. Hans eventually became managing director of Louis Dreyfus in London.

On 20th June 1910 Hans married Daisy Sarah Catherine Jackson Rowland at Reynoldston, Glamorgan. Daisy was born in Swansea on 14th August 1886. Daisy, the daughter of Christopher and Sarah J Rowland, was one of seven children: Frank Seymour J, 1884, Fred J, 1889, Harold J, 1891, Christopher J, 1894, Violet, 1896, and Stanley J, 1898. When they were first married Hans and Daisy lived in Hull. Daisy gave birth to her first child, a boy, while they were here. The son only lived three days.

It was when they married that Hans started using the name John Muller-Rowland. It was not until 25th February 1924 that Hans Muller officially became John

Muller-Rowland, changing his name by Deed Poll which was executed, attested, and enrolled in the Central Office of The Supreme Court of Judicature. Notification appeared in the London Gazette dated 7th March 1924.

In 1911, Louis Dreyfus was the India and England agent for the Royal Commission of wheat

Daisy

supplies of which Hans was a manager. Between 1911 and 1915 Hans and Daisy were living at Holmlea, Kutcherry Road, Karachi, India. Between June and September 1915 John was travelling back to Europe from India. After a short holiday in Switzerland and France he came to England, living in London, Liverpool and Hull. In April 1916 John's work took him to France, working in the head office of the firm in Paris, where he stayed until October 1918. It was while the family were living in Paris that Eric was born on 8th May 1917. The couple had six children, Daisie Frances Joyce, (known as Joy to the family), born on 12th December 1915 in Chelsea. Joan Veronica, born on 25th February 1919 in Streatham. Twins John Stuart and Stanley born on 27th November 1921 in Woking, and Wendy. All the children except for Wendy were officially born and registered with the name Muller, Rowland being added after John's naturalisation.

In July 1921, with Daisy pregnant with the twins, John's work took him back to Karachi. Daisy had two more boys while they were in India, the first one died at a few months old and the second was thirteen months old when he died. In 1921 John applied for naturalisation and British Nationality. A long-drawn-out process was to follow with reports from referees, the police checking the credentials of the referees and finally approval from the Home Office. Referees for Hans were Mr Ernest Capel Cure, Mr Joseph Fergusson Fawcett, and Mr Joseph Rank (of Ranks the grain merchants and millers). On 24th and 25th April 1922 a notice was published in The Times to the effect that he had applied for British nationality. British nationality was granted in April 1922.

Looking at John's passport gives an idea of how his work took him all over the world. Apart from Europe, the Far East was an important market for the company. In 1931 his passport permitted him to travel to all countries in Europe including the USSR, Turkey, Palestine, Iraq, Iran, and Egypt. In 1937, John was in Bangkok and his passport was endorsed by the British Consulate for him to travel to China, Japan, Siam, French Indochina, and the Dutch East Indies.

For the sake of this chapter, I will not concentrate on Eric, Stanley, or John (known as Stuart to the family) as they have their own chapters.

The Muller-Rowland family sailed to Karachi, India, (now Pakistan), on board the Kaiser I Hind (tonnage of 5989.30 with 529 passengers under the command of the ship's master, W B Palmer) of the Peninsular and Oriental Steam Navigation Company leaving London on 15th October 1920. The family is listed as John (39,) his wife Daisy (34), daughters Daisy (5), Joan (1) and son Eric (3), travelling with the family was Mrs Rosali Equi, nurse aged 51, and governess, Elsa de Bondeli aged 22. John was listed as a grain merchant. His country of last residence was given as Switzerland and nationality British.

Again in 1936 I find John and Daisy leaving the UK. Listed as Muller-Rowland with no first names. Daisy is shown as 43 years of age, being born in 1893 and John is listed as 47 years of age, being born in 1889 – both appear to be discrepancies on the passenger list. Daisy was sailing to Genoa, Italy whereas John was sailing to Colombo, Ceylon. Departing from Southampton as part of a party of 142 passengers, on 12th February 1936 on board a ship called the *Scharnhorst*, (not to be confused with the battleship of the same name). A ship of 10718.50 tons, operated by the Nord Deutscher Lloyd Bremen line under the command of ship's master W Stein. The eventual destination was to Yokohama, Japan. Having travelled through Italy to the South of France, Daisy returned to England on 27th, having boarded the ship in Marseilles.

The staff of Lord Dreyfus and John (Hans) Muller-Rowland in Karachi

During his time overseas, John contracted cerebral malaria which was to cause him problems with recurring bouts for the rest of his life. It was in 1939, while John was working in Paris, he took ill and was admitted to hospital where he remained for some considerable time before being moved to a nursing home where he died in 1939, at the age of 57. It was said that John's death was due to complications with uncontrolled hypertension. The whole family were in Paris to visit him a week or two before his death, all but Daisy and Joan were sent back to Horsell. Daisy and Joan remained at John's side.

John had lived in Horsell, Woking for nearly twenty years and paid great attention to the welfare of the neighbourhood. He was in the grain trade and was a prominent member of the Baltic exchange and an underwriter at Lloyds. John took a keen interest in agriculture. He bought Whapshott Farm which later consisted of Scotchers Farm, Shaws, and Young Stroat Farms, on Horsell Common. The farm comprised a XVIth Century farmhouse with four cottages, fifty-nine acres of mainly pastureland on which John had a small, long established herd of Guernsey cows, which he had bought in Cornwall and then had moved by train to Woking. Once the cows and two bulls had arrived in Woking, they were driven along the roads to Horsell Common. There was a dairy at the farm and John established a milk round in the locality. On the farm he also kept pigs, chickens, and geese. As well as livestock arable crops were grown, and Joan recalled the ploughing done with horses. There were also several acres of potatoes and soft fruit grown.

In the early 1930s, Emile, now penniless, moved from Portuguese East Africa to Horsell where he took up the post of farm secretary for John. When the farm was sold by the family in 1949, ten years after John's death, the agents added that there were a further 12 acres which was described as productive arable land.

I found while researching this book that Scotchers Farmhouse, and Barn became Grade 2 Listed Buildings in 1984.

As president of the Chobham Agricultural Society John gave many speeches about farming conditions at their annual dinners. He and his wife worked hard for the community with John providing the funds to purchase the Horsell Sports Ground and sought to preserve the countryside by helping the Horsell Commons Preservation Society. He was also a member of the local church and vice-president of the Horsell Amateur Dramatic Society. John spent many hours on the former

Church Hill House

Woking Unemployment Committee and his last chari-
table interest was the Woking Hospital Building Fund.

John bought Church Hill House, Horsell, a large family
home with plenty of room for the family to grow up, the
boys had the countryside all around them and they were
able to go off by themselves as they got older. Life at
Church Hill House obviously suited the family. John
embraced the lifestyle to become the country gent, he
could pursue his farming interests, he could involve
himself in the community and moreover the family
growing up had the freedom the countryside had to
offer. John by all accounts was by no means totally
committed to his work, whether it was his farming,
community work or his actual work. He always made
time for his family and was clearly devoted to them – he
also had a sense of fun.

The family had horses – all of them could ride but it is
said that John was not a particularly good horseman.
The family also had dogs – a Great Dane by the name of

Mike gets a mention as being a favourite. Life sounded idyllic – or some might say privileged – for the children, but I do not believe it was by any means a spoilt childhood. A testament to this is, Joan used to tell her children that that they never got pocket money while growing up at Church Hill House and they all had to do jobs on the farm to earn their money. The boys kept ferrets and used to go out catching rabbits. They enjoyed shooting and when it was time to slaughter the pigs the boys would get involved. The whole family enjoyed the joyrides offered by Alan Cobham's Flying Circus when it was in the area, and with Brooklands Motoring and Aviation Museum close by the boys would visit. It was obviously these events that provided the boys with their interest in aviation and cars.

A gardener by the name of Everett worked for the family. He doubled up as a chauffeur and spent time with the boys, there is a photograph of him helping with fixing a motorbike and side car that belonged to Stuart and Stanley. A cook and a couple of maids and a rather fiery nanny who originated from Brittany and only spoke French, wore traditional Breton clothing. With the Swiss family background and French nanny, it is not surprising that the children could all speak French. (This mentioned in Stuart's service records). Wendy says that she could speak French before she could speak English.

John also had a house at Selsey, Sussex, where the family would spend their holidays. They had a small boat, so no doubt spent a lot of time on that. John and Daisy would let the older children ride their ponies from Horsell to Selsey, camping on the way. Naturally, visits to Switzerland played an important part in the lives of the family, visiting relatives. Skiing and skating were some of the pastimes that they all took part in. Even post-war Stuart had a ski pass when still serving in the RAF.

John described his twins as mischievous and adventurous, often taking advantage of being identical twins and swapping identities. Eric was described as far more serious. By all accounts he wanted to study medicine. During the late 1930s, with war looking ever more likely, John became increasingly worried about his sons and what future they might have. He used to say, "Hitler will decide it for us".

A large congregation at John's funeral included many representatives of major businesses that he had been involved with in his working life, many of these household names of the day and some that are still well known. Many of the local organisations that John was involved with were well represented and many others that he might not have had a direct interest in. Over 100 wreaths from these organisations completed the day.

Eric (centre) and the twins

A couple of anecdotal stories about John, it was said that if his train was not due to stop at Woking, he would pull the communication cord and stop the train, and pay the fine of £5, another is that when in Switzerland he would stand on the platform chatting until the very last moment, just as the train was about to pull out of the station, driving Daisy mad. Finally, there is a story of him hold the children upside down over crevasses to pick gentians. These are handed down stories so may not be entirely accurate but there must be some basis for them.

It seems that Daisy was a strong woman and quite independent. Daisy was able to take herself and the children off on trips, such as a driving tour of Normandy and Brittany in an Austin Seven Swallow. Unfortunately, Daisy does not give the names of the children she took with her. Leaving Horsell at 1540 on 7th March 1930 the mileage on the car read 1735. The car was loaded on to the vessel at Southampton while Daisy went for dinner at the South Western Hotel. Daisy then returned to the ship ready to sail for Le Havre. In her notes she says that she had driven 58 miles from Horsell to Southampton. Daisy arrived in France at 0630 the next morning, her car was the first to be off loaded and Daisy then went off on her tour. It must be remembered that at the time of the journey cars had to be loaded and off loaded by crane at the ports – there were no roll on roll off ferries in 1930. Her notebook goes into much detail about the places she visited. The trip took in such places as Bayeux, Caen, and Mont St Michel. She visited many people she knew and many places of interest. Daisy returned to Woking on 23rd March having covered 849 miles. Other notebooks detail trips to Switzerland in the car and two more give details of a journey to India and one to South America!

John was not the only member of the family to immerse himself in local affairs, Daisy also got involved. Taking an interest in the local community, she was a member of the Women's Institute. Daisy became County President for Surrey, a role she obviously enjoyed with its many activities. She was heavily involved in Operation Produce that, with her late husband's farming interests put in an advantageous position. With the war only being over for four years and rationing still in place, produce from gardens and allotments created a vast amount of food which WI members were able to sell to supplement what was grown commercially. The Women's Institute played an important part in wartime. Daisy relinquished her post as County President in early 1949, her last message to members being published in the January edition of Surrey WI News. This was not the last fanfare to mark Daisy's involvement with the WI, she suggested that an exhibition should be held. On Tuesday 25th October 1955, the exhibition was held in Dorking Halls, a showcase to show off the skills of the members. After three years of planning there were over 680 exhibits, ranging from crafts to practical everyday items. Gardening and homemade produce played an integral part. In the main hall there was even an ideal country house with rooms laid out. The exhibition was regarded as a miniature Ideal Home Exhibition – an Ideal Country Home. On the opening day over 700 people visited what Daisy had proposed three years earlier.

On the 1939 Register Daisy J C Muller-Rowland is widowed and living at 1 Inwood, Pyrford Road, Woking with her daughter Daisie F J and two other members of her family. Daisy had a Parlour Maid, Minnie A Honour born on the 15th of July 1888, Elizabeth Honour, born on 11th March 1894, Cook and Margarette Averabach (Trepler) born in 1909 who worked as House Maid.

Daisy died on 12th February 1975. She had been living at Cedar Cottage, Little Heath Road, Chobham. Daisy was without doubt a loving mother and extremely proud of her family's achievements, having access to her newspaper cuttings album goes to prove this point. Dated 18th January 1946, a letter from the Central Chancery of The Orders and Knighthoods arrived in the post, this was the invitation for Daisy to attend the Investiture at Buckingham Palace to receive Stanley's DFC and Bar from His Majesty the King on Tuesday 12th February. Widowed at the age of fifty-two with the loss of two brothers during the First World War, a cousin and two sons during the Second World War and Stuart in 1950, Daisy also lost two granddaughters tragically young in accidents. Despite her hardships she remained positive and did not dwell on the past. Daisy's sense of faith and duty enabled her to get on with life. It is obvious this was continued with her children who committed their lives to duty. This extraordinary lady was admired

and respected by the whole family and by all that she had dealings with. In her will it was Daisy's wish that the boy's medals should be interred with her, which does seem to be the case.

Daisy Frances Joyce, known to the family as Joy and the oldest child, married Reginald Wallis "Charles" Mason, a chartered accountant, on 6th June 1942. They were both stationed at Bovington Camp, Dorset, Where Reginald

Joy Muller-Rowland

was a training officer in the Royal Tank Regiment and Joy was working as a Voluntary Aid Detachment (VAD) Nurse. Joy and Reginald met when he was in hospital with pneumonia.

Joan Veronica, born in February 1919 shows up on the 1939 Register as living at 9-10 Brunswick Square, London. She is listed as a medical student. This accommodation was for medical students as there were several of them at this address. Joan was doing her training at the Royal Free Hospital, Gray's Inn Road, London, the only London Hospital to provide medical training for women.

At the outbreak of war, Joan had become a clinical student which meant she was working on the wards and studying the different specialities of medicine. Joan

Joan Muller-Rowland

spent most of her time working in London during the Blitz. When Joan was on duty, with the nightly bombings, the staff and students used to sleep in the basement. In her memoires, Joan recounts how the staff used to go up on the hospital roof to watch the bombing of the City of London. The bombing became more sporadic as the early months of 1941 waned, although Joan recounts assisting with an operation on a junior doctor who had been in Holborn when her bus had been hit and was suffering from severe chest wounds.

Joan qualified as a doctor in 1942 and at some point, moved to the St Hellier Hospital in South London. Joan does not give the dates, but the hospital received two direct hits which killed two patients and several nurses that were just coming on duty. The safest place to be, as this was the strongest part of the hospital was the lift shaft. Joan, along with the night sister stayed there.

Later in the war, the doctors were working under extremely difficult circumstances when the Flying Bombs (Doodle Bugs) started raining down on London and the South East. On one occasion, Joan, working as a house surgeon, was operating on a patient when a doodle bug dropped on a building next to the hospital and despite the best efforts of the staff, dust and debris fell into the open wound. Joan was conscripted into the Royal Army Medical Corps in 1945. I have found the British Army Lists for 1945 where Joan is listed as Miss J V Muller-Rowland. In another list of 1946, she shows up under the heading of Women Officers Employed with the Royal Army Medical Corps. Commissioned under the Women's Forces (Officers Commissions) order 1941. She holds the rank of Lieutenant dated 20th January 1946.

One of Joan's early postings was to Ostend and then Bruges, working in a military hospital. It rather appears that this was a Canadian Military Hospital. It was while she was in Bruges that Joan met Richard Powell, a dental surgeon. He had been posted there, having served most of his time in Egypt and North Africa, proving the very necessary dental treatment with mobile dental units of the Royal Army Dental Corps. It seems that life was relatively good in Bruges at the time. The Germans had left some well stocked cellars of wine. Joan was treating wounded and recuperating soldiers in a hospital that had previously been a convent and is now a hotel. The officer's mess was, before the liberation, the German officer's mess. When Richard was released from the army, he returned to London to continue his practice there. Joan was posted to the British Military Hospital in Hamburg for a few months until she was finally de-mobbed.

In an army list of 1946, it shows that Joan had been promoted to Captain. Joan married Richard Pearce "Dick" Powell, dental surgeon, in the 3rd quarter of 1946 in St Mary's Church, Horsell. As her father had died, it was Stuart that gave her away. After the Second World War Joan became a GP. Dick died in 1985 at the age of 70 and Joan died in 2005 at the age of 86.

Born at 29 Cleveland Gardens, Paddington on 29th October 1928, Wendy shows up on the passenger list for a ship called the *Orcades*, a vessel of 14029.44 tons of the Orient Line under the command of C Fox, the ships master. Miss W Muller-Rowland, aged 11, left Southampton on the 2ndJuly 1940 bound for Adelaide, Australia. She was being evacuated to live with relatives. Wendy returned at the age of 17. When she arrived home her mother and sister did not recognise her.

Being away in Australia for the duration of the war, Wendy knew little about events that happened at home. Wendy went on to attend dances at Farnborough with her brother Stuart – this being the first time that she really had chance to get to know him. The boys had all been away at boarding school and being seven years younger than the twins she was always left out of things.

Wendy married, sub-mariner, Commander Thomas Charles Walker at Horsell Church, near Woking on 4th April 1953.

In Eric's chapter I refer to him joining the Territorial Army, for the sake of fitting it in I will give some small detail here. Along with his cousin, Frank Christopher Kenneth Rowland he joined the City of London Yeomanry before joining the Honourable Artillery Company.

194658, Captain Frank Christopher Kenneth Rowland, Croix de Guerre avec Palme, was the son of Daisy's brother Frank Seymour Jackson Rowland and Hannah Beatrice Rowland of Horsell, Surrey. Sometime after the death of his father, the family moved from Swansea to Horsell. Frank was employed by his uncle who was working for Louis Dreyfus at the time and worked alongside his cousin Eric. Frank had joined the Honourable Artillery Company as a Gunner, 1431426 in 1938, and was embodied into A Battery on 2nd September 1939. He was posted to 148 Field Regiment RA on 14th March 1940. Frank was discharged on 4th July 1941 to take up his commission and was appointed 2nd Lieutenant the following day. He was serving in 140 Field Regiment Royal Artillery when he was killed on 10th May 1943 at the age of 28. Frank is buried Medjez-el-Bab War Cemetery, Tunisia.

Daisy lost two brothers during the First World War. The first, P/S10744, Private Frank Seymour Jackson, 12th Battalion, Royal Fusiliers. Frank died in hospital in Boulogne, on 4th September 1916 having been wounded at the Somme. Son of Christopher and Sarah Jane Rowland, husband of Hannah Beatrice Rowland of 10

Preston Avenue, Newport, Monmouthshire, he served in the 12th Battalion, Royal Fusiliers. He is buried at Terlincthun British Cemetery, Wimille. Frank was one of the witnesses at the marriage of Hans and Daisy.

The second brother to lose his life was 2nd Lieutenant Stanley Jackson Rowland of the 3rd Battalion, Royal Welsh Fusiliers. Stanley was killed in Palestine on 2nd November 1917, he is buried at the Gaza War Cemetery.

Apart from the two brothers that were killed during the First World War, Daisy's three other brothers also served:

2nd Lieutenant, Harold Jackson Rowland joined the 7th (Cyclist) Battalion, Welsh Regiment on 8th June 1909, serving for just one year in this territorial unit. In 1913, Harold immigrated to Australia. Harold joined the 1st Pioneer Battalion of the 3rd Australian Infantry in March 1916. He fought with his regiment in France and was wounded in March 1918. Suffering the effects of gas, Harold was evacuated to hospital in England. In October 1918, Harold married Elsie Maud Webster in London. He returned to Australia in February 1919 and was discharged from the army in March. Harold died on 13th February 1927.

2nd Lieutenant, Christopher Rowland enlisted in the 2nd Battalion, The Royal Welsh Fusiliers, he was appointed a probationary 2nd Lieutenant along with his brother Stanley on 22nd May 1915. Christopher was wounded and medically discharged in 1917 and was awarded the Silver War Badge.

2nd Lieutenant, Fred Jackson Rowland, Royal Welsh Fusiliers. Unfortunately, I have not been able to find out more at the time of going to print.

Scharnhorst

The SS Scharnhorst that John and Daisy sailed on was launched in 1934 and completed in 1935 in time for her maiden voyage on 8th May 1935. Operated by the Norddeutscher Lloyd Line she was the first large passenger liner built by the Third Reich. She was named after General Gerhard J D von Scharnhorst and was to operate on the Far East route from Bremen to Yokohama. During a voyage in 1937, when the Japanese had invaded China the crew of Scharnhorst rescued several Chinese fishermen that had been attacked by a Japanese ship. At the outbreak of the Second World War Scharnhorst was in Kobe.

As she belonged to one of the belligerent nations and in the port of a then neutral country she was impounded. During 1940/41 work started to convert her into a warship, this came to a stop after the Battle of Midway in 1942 and work then commenced to convert her into a much-needed escort carrier for the Japanese Navy, that had lost a number of these in the Battle of Midway. Once work was completed, she put to sea on 15th November 1943 as His Imperial Japanese Majesty's Ship Shinyo. The compliment was 32 aircraft, and the job was to escort convoys in the Yellow Sea and trade routes in the area. While escorting a convoy bound for Singapore on 17th November 1944 the convoy was sighted by the crew of the submarine USS Spadefish. To take advantage of the element of surprise the Captain, Gordon Waite Underwood Spadefish remained submerged and shadowed the convoy until night fall. Outrunning the convoy, the Spadefish turned to attack. Firing six torpedoes at the Shinyo he quickly turned and fired another four torpedoes at the tankers in the convoy. Some of the torpedoes struck the Shinyo on the starboard side rupturing her fuel bunkers which caught fire. By the nature of the fact, she was a carrier she had a great amount of aviation fuel on board which soon exploded along with the ammunition. Listing to starboard very quickly she was engulfed in flame and sunk with her entire crew of 942.

RMS Orcades.

The Orcades was built in 1936 to operate the Britain-Australia-New Zealand route as a Mail Ship. In 1939 she was requisitioned by the British Government as a troopship, becoming HMS Orcades. As part of the conversion, she received armament. In 1941 the Orcades was trooping to the Halifax, Nova Scotia, with British troops bound for Singapore. These men changed to another vessel on arriving in Halifax. In February 1942 Orcades was evacuating RAF personnel, non-essential troops and wounded from Java in front of the Japanese invasion.

(Author's note, the uncle of Steve Lane of Libri was one of the troops in 1941).

On 9th October 1942 she set sail from Cape Town, bound for Liverpool with 741 passengers plus crew, 3000 tons of cargo, and 2000 bags of mail. At about 1028hrs on the 10th when she ws approximately 220 nautical miles south west of Cape Town, she was attacked by the U172, commanded by Kapitanleutnant Carl Emmerman. Emmerman fired two torpedoes which hit home, damaging the ship. It took another five torpedoes to sink her. In the meantime, the gunners on board Orcades fired at the U Boat. The Orcades finally sank at 1300hrs. With the time it took to sink her the passengers and most of the crew managed to abandon ship. The Polish ship, GRT Narwik arrived on the scene and performed a daring rescue operation in the face of the possibility of further sub marine attacks A total of 1022 survivors were plucked from the lifeboats. It was a miracle that only 45 lives were lost.

From the Family 2

My memories of the boys are not that clear because I was seven years younger than the twins. Being the youngest child and a girl, I was left out of some of the things they got up to. I do remember that Eric was good friends with his cousin Frank, whose mother, Auntie Bea had moved to Woking from Wales. I adored the twins. I recall that Stuart played his cards close to his chest, whereas Stanley was a hoot, who, like our father, he could laugh about his mistakes. For twins, the two boys had totally different personalities.

Wendy

Stuart and Wendy

CHAPTER 2

The Mediterranean and North Africa

The early part of the war in North Africa was conducted by the British and Commonwealth forces against the Italians. The Italian forces had been driven from the border of Egypt and into Libya. To assist in dislodging the British from the region and so secure the much-needed oil supplies, Germany sent in its Afrika Korps. Although they had not previously fought in North Africa or the desert the advantage still lay with them. They were led by General Erwin Rommel, a veteran of the First World War and brilliant tactician. The Germans had far superior tanks, artillery, and anti-tank gun crews. With the air force, Rommel worked his forces in a combined effort. With his great drive and personality, Rommel began to achieve results that the Italians had not been able to. He succeeded in pushing the British back into Egypt by April 1941, just four months after arriving in the region. This left a pocket at Tobruk still in British hands.

Britain had had interests in the Middle East for many years so could gain some of the supplies needed from that area whereas the Axis forces had to rely on nearly all being shipped from Europe across the Mediterranean. This meant running the gauntlet with the Royal Navy and Royal Air Force. As for Britain, these issues could be resolved without using the Mediterranean as a supply route. Armaments, ammunition, and food supplies could be taken via the Cape and up the Suez Canal and from there they could use the railway from Cairo. Some of the fuel could be obtained in the region while water could be supplied by pipeline from Egypt.

A system, called the Trans-African Staging Route, had been set up, whereby parts of aircraft were taken to Takoradi on the Gold Coast where they would be re-assembled and ferried to Egypt. Leaving Takoradi the pilots would fly to Shallufa, near Cairo via Kano, Maiduguri, El Fasher, Khartoum, Luxor, and on to Cairo. This was quite often done by new crews as this was also a major disembarkation port for them. Others were taken by tour-expired crews awaiting further postings.

For the pilots who had a remote interest in the past this would have been one massive history lesson, seeing things they had read about in books but never having dreamt that they would get to see them from the air. Alternatively, goods and personnel would be flown direct from Britain via Gibraltar by ferry pilots or new crews and in some cases entire squadrons would collect new aircraft and fly them out.

Although some of the Axis supplies could be flown in this would not be sufficient to sustain the huge requirement for materials and men. Therefore, the Germans and Italians had to rely on shipping. The Italian ports of Naples, Brindisi, Taranto, and Bari were the major hubs for this operation. These ports would be subjected to the attentions of the RN and RAF due to their importance. At sea, the convoys again would be vulnerable to attack from submarines, surface vessels and from the air.

Vital to the British was the island of Gibraltar, sitting at the entrance to the Mediterranean and the British island of Malta. Sitting south of Sicily, Malta had airfields from which the RAF could mount attacks on enemy convoys as well as give air cover for inbound British convoys. The Grand Harbour at Valletta, the island's capital provided the RN with a depot for its ships and submarines. This island, vital to both powers was later to suffer terrible poundings by both the Germans and Italians.

For those convoys that crossed the sea unscathed their troubles were not over. The nearest point for the Axis to land the supplies was Libya. Libya had three major ports, Tripoli being the main one, Benghazi, which regularly received heavy attention from the RAF and Tobruk which was in British hands, leaving only two viable. Once unloaded the convoys then had to return across the Mediterranean, running the gauntlet once more.

Supplies that had reached these ports had to be moved east to the front in Egypt. With no railway the only two options were to use small coasters and move them by sea, which again proved vulnerable to attacks from the RN and RAF, or to move them by the only road in trucks. Transporting the materials by 2-ton trucks over 1000 miles used a substantial amount of the fuel that had to be delivered. The trucks themselves would make easy targets for the RAF and Long-Range Desert Groups (LRDG). As Rommel pushed the British further back so the supply lines became longer compounding the problem. Stretching their supply lines was one problem that Germany had historically suffered, during the First World War and the invasion of the Low Countries in 1940.

With the arrival of General Auchinleck in Egypt things started to turn against the Afrika Korps. He launched his offensive, Operation Crusader on 18th November 1941. The Germans and Italians suffered the loss of 19 vital supply ships in October and 7 on 9th November which included 15,500 tons of much needed fuel.

The state of the air forces in the region was roughly equal, with approximately 320 German and 300 Italian aircraft pitched against the RAF's 660 in Egypt plus a further 120 in Malta.

By the beginning of December, with his supplies desperately short, Rommel was forced to retreat. Once ground had been re-taken the damage inflicted by the RAF and LRDG became apparent. Numerous aircraft had been wrecked on airfields and many more had been shot down in the desert, making a total loss of 458 aircraft. The LRDG had made a good show of themselves destroying lines of communication and raiding airfields and supply dumps.

By the end of December, the tables had turned in Rommel's favour, as the British supply lines were now stretched. Unseen by the defenders on Gibraltar nineteen U-Boats slipped into the Mediterranean from the Atlantic. The aircraft carrier *HMS Ark Royal* fell prey to one of these on 13th November and twelve days later a battleship was sunk. The Italians, with two midget sub-marines sent two more battleships to the bottom.

In December much needed supplies for Rommel's Afrika Korps started to arrive as a convoy with a large naval escort, docked in Tripoli. In early December, the Germans had succeeded in sinking one battleship and one cruiser of the Royal Navy. Another battleship and cruiser were damaged. With these ships out of the equation the supply convoys had an easier passage. At the beginning of January 1942, five ships arrived in Tripoli under a naval escort. This brought 12,500 tons of ammunition, over 15,000 tons of fuel, 650 vehicles and 900 troops. Additionally, 400 aircraft had arrived on Sicily, the great air battle to knock out British interests in Malta could now begin. With fresh supplies arriving and shorter distances to transport them Rommel was able to mount an attack. The British troops were taken by surprise on 21st January.

After the initial German successes, there followed four months in which the battle stagnated. The ground forces hardly moved. On the other hand, the air forces kept up their offensives. With the additional aircraft based in Sicily the attacks on Malta increased. It got to the point where at the end of March the RAF fighter element had been taken down to just a handful of aircraft, with the bomber force faring little better. This constant battering of the airfields hindered the ground crews, as servicing became extremely difficult with daily bombing. A shortage of spares led to some aircraft becoming unserviceable, and those that were serviceable frequently suffered from engine failures.

With the German U Boats operating and the increased Axis air power British convoys bound for Malta struggled to get through. With its prominent position, Malta faced the threat of invasion, although this was called off due to pressure on the Eastern Front and the RAF's mass raids on German towns and cities. Resources were re-deployed from the Mediterranean and North Africa to counter these issues.

Rommel's forces had been receiving plentiful supplies for the first half of the year. The British anti-shipping force on Malta was much depleted and the loss of RN ships, meant the Axis convoys had a much clearer run. Meanwhile the British supplies kept coming via the Cape.

Rommel renewed his offensive on 26th May 1942 having built up his army and sufficient supplies. Pushing east, the Afrika Korps took Tobruk on 21st June, and it came with a huge bonus. A gold mine of British stocks, 1,500,000 gallons of fuel, 3,000,000 field rations, water, clothing, tinned food, beer, whiskey, and a vast stock of desert boots, far superior to those issued to his own troops. It seemed inevitable that Rommel would take Egypt. What he had not bargained for was the tenacity of the Eighth Army, who stopped him at El Alamein. The Luftwaffe had failed to keep up with the army giving the RAF the opportunity to keep up the pressure on the Axis troops with round the clock attacks. Once more Rommel's force had reached the point where it was difficult to keep enough supplies coming to continue their offensive.

With reinforcements of more Spitfires, Beauforts and Beaufighters in Malta the balance started to change. Enemy attacks became less frequent and those that did take place met more resistance. The greater number of aircraft also enabled better convoy protection for Malta-bound convoys. With more British firepower the Axis convoys started to suffer heavy losses once more.

It should also be mentioned that besides the brave efforts of the bomber and fighter pilots there were the reconnaissance aircraft whose pilots and crews often flew alone over long distances and for long periods of time. Their role was equally important in the battle to prevent supplies getting through. The cracking of the Enigma code at Bletchley Park also had a major role to play. Signals concerning shipping, giving details of sailing times, cargoes, names of ships and ports of embarkation, were being deciphered and the messages passed to the forces in the Mediterranean and North Africa. The pilots could often go straight to the position of the convoy. The pilots did not know how this happened but were very aware that something was going on. Not only did Bletchley provide shipping information, but they could also tell the commanders in the field the exact disposition of the Afrika Korps.

Fuel was to be the major stumbling block for the Axis forces. Germany had started producing synthetic oil from coal to supplement its stocks of crude oil. Even this was not enough to meet the needs, consumption being greater than production. Italy did not have the facilities to produce the synthetic oil as it had no coal. The Italians had to greatly reduce its operations in the Mediterranean. The capital ships were laid up in the ports, where they would remain until the Italian surrender in September 1943.

The Germans had to curtail some of its operations in the North Sea for the same reason. In the few weeks prior to the Battle of El Alamein only half the supply ships reached their destination. With the loss of so much shipping Rommel began to suspect that the British forces must have some prior knowledge of the sailings of these convoys. He did not entirely trust the Italians and suspected that there was some leaking of information to the British. On the British side members of the Eighth Army suspected something, as the new commander, General Montgomery, seemed to have an in-depth knowledge of the disposition of the Afrika Korps, their strengths and weaknesses, the positions of troops and armour and finally the dire situation for supplies.

On 23rd October 1942, a major bombardment of the German positions began. This was the start of Montgomery's offensive at El Alamein. Intelligence from Bletchley Park told him the Axis forces only had enough supplies to fight for four days. With a lack of spares the tanks were breaking down, with fewer than half the previous year's number still in service. The situation became so serious that a full-blown withdrawal was going to be difficult without the fuel required. On 2nd November Rommel sent a message to Berlin.

"The Army will no longer be in a position to prevent a further attempt by strong enemy forces to break through, which may be expected today or tomorrow. The stocks of ammunition still available are in the front area, while there are no stocks worth mentioning in the rear area. The tiny stocks of fuel do not permit a movement to the rear over great distances. On the single road available, the Army will certainly be attacked day and night by the RAF. In this situation, despite heroic resistance and the excellent spirit of the troops, the gradual annihilation of the Army must be faced."

Hitler responded by ordering a stand to the last man. To Rommel this was a sacrifice he was not prepared to take. Rommel asked Hitler for permission to withdraw. Before a reply was received, he had already put his plan into action. The retreat was underway. As the situation had become so serious, both the Italian and German air forces began to fly reinforcements and supplies in from Sicily. Inevitably the RAF mauled these in the same way that it had the shipping. It was not necessarily a one-sided affair as these transports carried defensive armament and the troop carriers had their occupants firing automatic weapons from the windows.

On 8th November 1942, the Anglo-American landings in Algeria took place. Operation Torch was to bring pressure to bear on the Axis forces from the west in addition to being pushed back from the east. Tobruk was retaken by the British on 13th November. The harbour had been the target of numerous raids by the RAF and by now the USAAF, consequently this was destroyed and unusable. The facilities were out of action and several sunken vessels in the entrance and in the harbour would have made entry impossible.

Driven back still further, Rommel tried to take advantage of the fact that on one part of the front at Kasserine, in the west, his troops faced an inexperienced American Division. His plan was to outflank the Allies and take the front line from behind. This was thwarted by the rapid deployment of reinforcements to the area.

Following Kasserine, Rommel's forces were driven further towards the coast in Tunisia. He had one more last ditch stand to try to reverse his fortunes in North Africa. Launching an offensive against Montgomery's forces at the Mareth Line, bitter fighting took place. The Eighth Army faced the onslaught and eventually won the battle. During his retreat, Rommel had been sending Allied POW's back to Italy in the returning ships. The Allies were aware of this and for that reason did not attack these vessels on the return voyage.

With only two ports available to him Rommel had to rely more on air transport for his supplies. The routes flown by the transport aircraft and the airfields would now be within range of the Spitfire Squadrons based in North Africa, so the lumbering transports stood little chance. The bomber Squadrons of the RAF also played their part in attacking the landing grounds. On 14th May 1943, the war in North Africa came to an end. The Axis forces had done their best to evacuate their troops, but this still led to the loss of 250,000 becoming POWs.

Loss Rates

A table drawn up in 1942 gave an indication of the dangers faced by RAF crews. It shows in detail the rough statistics of chances of survival. It does not make pleasant reading and was kept from public view as well as aircrews themselves.

	Percentage Chance of Survival	
	One Tour	Two Tours
1. Torpedo Bomber	17.5	3
2. Light Bomber	25.5	6.5
3. Fighter Reconnaissance	31	9.5
4. Night Fighter	39	15
5. Bomber Reconnaissance	42	17.5
6. Day Fighter	43	18.5
7. Heavy and Medium Bombers	44	19.5
8. Light General Reconnaissance Landplanes	45	20
9. Medium General Reconnaissance Landplanes	56	31.5
10. Long Range Fighter	59.5	35.5
11. Sunderland Flying Boat	66	43.5
12. Heavy General Reconnaissance	71	50.5
13. Catalina Flying Boat	77	60

To put this another way: three out of every one hundred airmen stood a chance of surviving two tours of operations on the low-level torpedo bombers, ninety-seven did not.

The table was produced to enable Training Command to assess the replacements that would be needed and how frequently this would have to happen. It came about by 1942 that the operational flying expectancy was as little as two months for the top category.

This table has been reproduced here to give perspective as all three brothers came into the top two categories. Many of the light and medium bomber squadrons came under Coastal Command on anti-shipping duties. As the reader will see in the following chapter, Eric and Stanley were members of Coastal Command. These operations were carried out at extremely low level over the sea. The risks to the crews flying this type of mission were extreme, there was always the probability of hitting the water, as happened to Eric.

Attacking shipping was dangerous because the chances of hitting masts was always present. Added to this, when a ship exploded it was common for aircraft to be hit and sometimes brought down by debris. Many of the convoys attacked were also surrounded by flak ships giving heavy anti-aircraft fire. During the time Eric and Stanley were flying in the anti-shipping role they were in Bristol Beauforts and Beaufighters. The Beaufighter was armed with torpedoes, rockets and/or cannon. Although he was mainly operating over land, Stuart still came into this category.

As described by Pierre Clostermann, a French Pilot who came to England and took part in numerous air battles, *"these units were made up of hardcore characters who threw themselves into the fray and kept returning. Anyone that took part in this type of operation knew the risks were high. It was common for losses to run at 75% per month."*

As will be seen later, the type of operations that Stuart was flying were of a similar nature, only most of his work was focused on the railways and rivers in Burma.

RAF Training

Training in the Royal Air Force during the 1930s was slow. Pilots were being trained but very few other crew members. In 1936, with the formation of the Royal Air Force Volunteer Reserve, pilots, observers, and wireless operators received training in their spare time. By the outbreak of war in 1939 there were 10,000 men in the

RAFVR in the three categories. In the regular service wireless operators and air gunners were mostly volunteers from the ground trades within the organisation. In December 1939, the training schemes for pilots were set up in Canada, New Zealand and Australia with the training staff made up of RAF instructors. The main problem they faced was a lack of instructors, especially those with many hours of flying and operational experience. Commanders were reluctant to release their best crews for this purpose. Following suit Rhodesia and South Africa set up training schools under the same guidelines. Other aircrew trades had to be trained in Britain, but it was not until 1921 that these trades were taught in the overseas schools. Even the aircrews from these countries had to come to Britain to be trained before that date. In the USA General Arnold formed a similar establishment. The combined effort of the countries involved in the training plan produced 11,000 pilots and 17,000 other aircrew in 1942.

Once trained in the respective countries as pilots they would normally return to the UK for further specialist training at the various schools dotted around. As was the case with Stanley especially, some of the best pupils were kept on at the SFTS to train other pilots. Although aircrew were conscripted to serve in the armed forces, aircrew duties were voluntary once the first process had taken place.

Many chose the RAF as this provided a great sense of adventure. In the wake of Dunkirk this was one of the few ways that Britain could strike back at Germany. These airmen had joined to fight so some, understandably, had grievances about having to stay on to be instructors when their fellow pupils were going off to join their squadrons. On the other hand, some saw this prolonged delay as somewhat safer than going into action. This situation might well have helped solve the shortage of instructors, with many very dedicated aircrews on hand to carry out this task. The length of this process is illustrated by the long period between Stanley finishing torpedo training and finally becoming operational.

As war progressed the training system grew to accommodate the developing needs of the service with Air Observers Navigation Schools, Bombing and Gunnery and Advanced Bombing and Gunnery Schools. Those selected as wireless operators went to Wireless School then on to Bombing and Gunnery courses. The School of General Reconnaissance and Torpedo Schools were those that particularly come into the story of Eric, Stanley, and Stuart. Operational Training Units were set up around the country and overseas to prepare crews for their imminent postings to operational squadrons. An unfortunate side effect of the OTUs is that in many cases pilots were given charge of aircraft that had more power than those they had previously trained on. Accidents were also frequent as a result of the unreliability of the heavily used and sometimes war weary aircraft they had to fly in. An example of this was when Stuart was at 70 OTU when he made a forced landing in the desert.

The question of recognition also came about with the need to recognise our own aircraft and those of the enemy. For the anti-shipping and convoy protection units of Coastal Command it was necessary to be able to identify ships at range and quickly. Once airborne radar became available a whole new trade was required and training schools had to be set up to cater for this. Apart from the formal schools and the prescribed methods of teaching, new tactics had to be developed and this is where experienced pilots would come into the system. It shows that some had a particular skill in studying the tactics used and developed new ways to improve this. Continuation training on the squadron became a familiar thing. Crews arriving would be taken out to familiarise themselves with the area of operations and to be brought up to date with any recent changes. They also had to learn the squadrons approach to operations.

As the war progressed the number of pilots increased dramatically, enabling the RAF to expand and replace pilots as required. In Europe, the Axis powers had no such facility, having to rely on home produced aircrew. As the war turned against them, Germany and her allies had the added factor of fuel shortages which meant they could not afford to use in training what was sorely needed for combat.

Although commonly called a rest tour, a posting to an OTU was not necessarily the case. New pilots coming from SFTS would be flying more powerful aircraft. Very few of the aircraft used in the OTU's had dual control. The risk for the instructors, both pilots and other crew members was that should these inexperienced pilots lose control of the aircraft there was little the instructors could do to rectify the problem. Many aircraft were lost at OTUs in this way. In the case of the Bristol Beaufighter the instructor pilot stood behind the pupil so could not reach the controls if something did go wrong. The number of new aircrews arriving at the OTUs differed from time to time, this did enable the instructors some time off. At the OTUs pilots and aircrew flew and ate together, they shared the same bar facilities giving them the chance to get to know each other and to form their own crews. It was obviously essential that they got on with each other when they started operations. Once finished at OTU the crews would be posted to operational squadrons.

Aircrews flying in operations were issued with an escape kit, usually worn in a belt. In this they would have a map of the relevant area, some local currency, and benzedrine tablets. This was then adapted by the crews to their individual likes. A dinghy was stowed in the wing of the aircraft in case of being shot down in the sea. In the dinghy was stowed some tins of water and basic rations, which largely depended on what was available. For the aircrews operating in the desert there was the "Goolie Chit" a note that could be shown to anyone who happened to rescue downed airmen. This was a promise by the British government to reward them if the crew were handed over safely to the British authorities or returned them to the British military.

CHAPTER 3

Eric Muller-Rowland

Eric, the second child of Hans and Daisy was born on 8th May 1917 in the parish of St Bland, Paris. He was a Swiss citizen at birth and became a British citizen on 31st October 1922.

He was educated at Sunnydown School, Hog's Back near Guildford and went on to board at Uppingham School, Rutland, from January 1931 to December 1935. He was a member of West Bank House. While he was at Uppingham, Eric was in the Junior Division of the Officer Training Corps. Eric gained his Certificate A, fulfilling the necessary conditions of efficient service and qualified in the Infantry syllabus examinations. This entitled him, if he so wished or the need arose, to gain a commission in the Supplementary Reserve, Territorial Army or the Territorial Reserve of Officers of the Active Militia of Canada. As a Dominion of the British Empire, many British citizens emigrated to Canada. Those that were eligible could serve in the Canadian forces or be liable to call up should the need arise. This also meant that in the event of a national emergency and the mobilization of the Regular Army and/or Territorial Army, Eric was to immediately provide his contact details to the War Office. This document was dated 5th March 1935.

In July, Eric attained his School Certificate A, having studied Scripture Knowledge, English, History, Geography, Latin, French, Mathematics, Physics,

Eric in civilian clothes

Chemistry, Music and Drawing, he passed with a credit in English and French (written and oral). In December, Eric attained credits in Scripture Knowledge, English, History, French, both written and oral, and elementary Mathematics.

Eric had an interest in aviation during the 1930s, taking his first flying lesson on 9th March 1936 in De Havilland 60 Gypsy Moth G-ABTS from Brooklands. After flying the DH 82 Tiger Moth and DH85 Leopard Moth, Eric's aviator's certificate, No13748 was issued on 15th April 1936. It appears that he never completed his training to achieve his Full Private Pilot's Licence, his last flight being on 28th July the same year.

It was 29th September 1938 when Eric joined the Territorial Army (T/A) and was embodied into the Honourable Artillery Company on 1st September 1939, as Gunner 1436875 in C Battery. On 13th September he was posted to 2 Regiment, B Battery and classified as a driver on 1st September 1940.

After nearly four years of service with the T/A, Eric transferred to the Royal Air Force, on 19th May 1941, his new number was 656511. The description of Eric on his service record shows he was 5ft 6 1/2ins, 32 1/2-inch chest, brown hair, and brown eyes with a fresh complexion. After completion of his basic training Eric started his flying training at No1 Elementary Flying Training School (EFTS), at the De Havilland School of Flying, Hatfield, Hertfordshire, on 28th July. Eric's elementary training took place in the D.H. Tiger Moth T5379. Taking into consideration that Eric had some previous experience he did his first solo flight on 4th August carrying out steep turns and climbing turns.

On 14th August Eric undertook his first Air Navigation training, his instructor was Senior Pilot Street. This flight he took was from Hatfield to Halton, Henlow and returning to Hatfield. With ever increasing numbers of solo flights building up in his logbook this pattern continued through August until the 31st when Chief Flying Instructor, Squadron Leader Pedley took him for his test. Brushing up on his skills between 31st August and 4th September he passed on 5th September with 27.40hrs dual flying and 33.05hrs solo, with an above average rating as a pilot. On 6th September Eric was signed off with 6hrs on the Link Trainer, again with an above average rating.

Under the British Commonwealth Air Training Plan, Eric's next move was to No 2 Squadron, 36 Service Flying Training School (SFTS) at RCAF Station, Penhold, Alberta, Canada. It was on October the 31st that he started his multi engine training on the Airspeed Oxford. His first solo flight came very soon afterwards on 7th November. Still only holding the rank of Leading Aircrafts Man, (LAC), Eric was certified to go on training flights with another pupil after 35 hours dual or solo on the Oxford. Eric's test for multi engine flying with the Chief Flying Instructor was taken on 17th January 1942 with his cross-country test on the on the 19th. Over the course of the next few days Eric flew as safety pilot for other cross-country flights.

Eric and Stuart in skiing gear

On 29th January, just the day before Eric was awarded his wings, he was discharged from the RAF and was commissioned as a Pilot Officer in the RAF Volunteer Reserve (RAFVR) with yet another service number, 122965. Eric had completed 25.40 hours daytime dual flying and 3.45 night along with 45.50 daytime and 7.10 night-time as pilot. His total flying hours at this point was 142.25. Again, Eric was assessed as above average. From here he went on to the General Reconnaissance School at Royal Canadian Air Force (RCAF) Station Charlottetown, Prince Edward Island. His training took place between 7th February and 10th April 1942 at No 32 Operational Training Unit, Patricia Bay, British Columbia, flying the Airspeed Oxford and Handley Page Hampden. At Patricia Bay, he carried out his training in bombing practice with the Hampden, this incorporated cross country flights, navigation training and night flying and bombing.

(Author's note; There were two different categories of commission in the RAF. A Permanent Commission was given to officers that intended to make a career in the service and men like Eric that had entered the RAF for the duration of the war and not intending to make their career

in the RAF were given a Short Service Commission in the Royal Air Force Volunteer Reserve).

On 18th June 1942 Eric was cleared to carry passengers and, on the 20th, he flew his first training missions with a full crew. The crew made up of Sergeants Mellor, McDonald and Leatham, would become Eric's regular crew until 31st January 1943. Initially they flew on cross country navigation flights followed on the 26th by practice bombing runs. It was on the 30th they got to drop practice, dropping bombs from 10000ft.

Air to air gunnery was another feature on this course along with air to ground. It appears from Eric's logbook that most of his bombing attacks were from low level with attacks on static and moving targets. Passing out from No32 Operational Training Unit (O.T.U) he was assessed as average with 168 hours as a pilot. Eric's low-level work was to lead him on to his next posting back in the UK at No 4 Torpedo Training Squadron, No5 O.T.U. at Turnberry. Flying the Hampden, Eric and his crew practiced low flying in preparation for dropping torpedoes. With targets travelling at a variety of speeds it was of great importance to assess the speed and deflection needed to hit the target. The crew became quite reliable with a hit rate of 60% by the end of the course. With 22.25 hrs flown. Eric's assessment as a pilot at the end of the course was Average+.

After his last fight with the Torpedo Training Squadron a rapid move was made when Eric was posted to 144 Squadron, again flying the Hampden, at Leuchars. His first few flights were local familiarisation and navigation exercises. Eric's first operation was on 17th December when he took part in a "Rover Patrol". A "Rover Patrol" was an unplanned patrol looking for targets as opposed to a strike which was a planned attack on a specific target. On trying to attack a motor vessel his torpedo

Eric on completion of his training (2nd from right on front row)

hung up so was forced to abort the attack. He returned to Lossiemouth having been diverted. An aircraft night flying test in two different aircraft was carried out on the 23rd, these being NV-S and NV-T. The navigator on both flights was Sergeant McDonald. Following on from this, with his normal crew in NV-O, Eric took part in a night strike on Lervic (Leirvik), a flying time of 6hrs 25mins.

On 4th January 1943, the Squadron was called on to conduct a search patrol, when in Hampden NV-B, Eric left Leuchars with his crew of Sergeants Mellor, McDonald and Leatham to take part. I cannot find any more information about the reason or outcome of this search.

A strike to Egero was planned for the 11th with 6 aircraft taking off from Sumburgh, having flown there from Leuchars the previous day. With thick cloud and rain Eric and his crew took off at 1655hrs. The pilot of one of the other aircraft deemed it too dangerous for low level flying. On approaching the target area there were no marker flares to be seen, the weather had closed in and with zero visibility the strike was abandoned. At 2005hrs Eric flew into a front of extremely bad weather which extended for over 70 miles. Eric and four other aircraft made it back to Leuchars safely with the sixth aircraft landing at Peterhead. The winter weather meant that operations were sometimes cancelled at short notice. Eric did not fly for the next four days.

With a full moon on the 16th Eric was airborne at 1550hrs. On arrival at the start point of his patrol it was 1810hrs, close to the Norwegian coast. At 1830hrs the crew sighted two search lights approximately 1-2 miles apart. Ineffective slightly heavy anti-aircraft fire was encountered but no enemy aircraft. Ending the patrol at 1854hrs he flew back to Scotland, landing at 2116hrs.

On the 18th the squadron made Rover patrols on the enemy in moonlight, the second of these being another attack on Lervic. On both occasions the aircraft were diverted to Lossiemouth. Towards the end of the month 144 converted to the Bristol Beaufighter MK IV. In preparation for this Eric was taken up for a demonstration in a Bristol Blenheim by Squadron Leader Gracy for the first flight on the 23rd, with Eric taking the controls for the next two flights that day and the following day.

Eric's first flights in the new Beaufighter were with Squadron Leader Gracy instructing, on the 26th, 27th, 28th. On 29th in JL610 NV-B, Eric flew with Squadron Leader Gracy in the morning, with Eric taking the controls in the afternoon and Squadron Leader Gracy assessing him. After his assessment flight, Eric flew solo in the Beaufighter. The whole of February was taken up with familiarising themselves with the new aircraft, conducting exercises and air to sea firing practice. Just as importantly, a couple of fuel consumption tests were flown.

Eric in uniform

It was when converting to the Beaufighter that Eric crewed up with Flight Sergeant Alexander. The first mission that Eric flew in the Beaufighter was a "Rover" patrol on 16th March, flying JL718 NV-D, with five other aircraft. Taking off at 1117hrs the formation set course for St Andrews where they rendezvoused with their escort from 235 Squadron. The patrol area was a few miles off the Norwegian coast. No shipping was sighted in time before the aircraft were recalled to base. All aircraft landed back at Leuchars at 1335hrs.

The following day Eric flew another Armed Rover in formation with other aircraft from 144, to Egero and Lister. Taking off at 1303hrs the formation set course for St Andrews with 10/10ths cloud above them, although visibility was reasonable beneath the cloud. About 50 miles from the Norwegian coast, they encountered haze which reduced visibility to 1000yds and less in places. On breaking from the haze, the coast could be seen about ten miles ahead. Turning south east they flew parallel with the coast, about 2 miles out.

144 Squadron photograph (Eric seated 3rd from right)

Two fishing boats and one larger vessel of approximately 150 tons were sighted with no action being taken. A larger fishing fleet was sighted and photographed by Eric's navigator, Flight Sergeant Alexander. No enemy opposition was encountered on this trip. The formation set course for base, again flying into haze for much of the journey. Eric dropped down to sea level with two other aircraft once they were about 30 miles from the coast. Making landfall at Arbroath they headed for Leuchars and landed at 1718hrs.

On 13th April Eric flew from Leuchars to Reykjavik, Iceland, (he does not state in his logbook what the reason was), he returned to base on the 16th.

An anti-submarine strike was carried out on the 19th with Eric flying to Sumburgh. Due to the extreme distance to be covered and length of the operation, it was necessary to re-fuel and attend the briefing for the operation before commencing to Norway. Operating at the endurance limits of the aircraft at times led to losses because of running out of fuel. If the pilot should need to make violent manoeuvres to avoid enemy action, he needed a reserve of fuel in order to get back to base. Reports differ in Eric's logbook and the Operational Record Book (ORB). Eric reports that he attacked a submarine with his cannons in harbour in Bergen, but the ORB has no mention of this. Six aircraft took part in this operation and some crews reported seeing at a distance, a submarine submerge but nothing more being sighted.

There was another "Rover" flown on the 24th to Lister-Egero again, but the next few days were taken up with training in fighter affiliation and fighter evasion exercises.

The next operation in Eric's logbook is a reconnaissance to Lista-Stavanger on 1st May. Flying Beaufighter VI NV-A

Eric took off independently from Tain at 1447hrs to fly to Wick, landing at 1510hrs. Here the squadron formatted with 28 other aircraft, including aircraft from 404 Squadron, and as fighter escort, 235 Squadron.

The Norwegian coast was sighted at 2020hrs and five minutes later three ME 109s were seen at about 500ft heading from the land at a range of about two miles. Two more were seen a couple of minutes later, formatting with the first three at about a mile range. One of the enemy aircraft dived on Eric's Beaufighter, with cannon firing, with hits sighted in the sea behind Eric's aircraft. Another 109 joined the attack on Eric. With Eric taking evasive action he turned steeply to port and the enemy aircraft overshot about 100yds away.

Ranging from 100ft to 700ft fifty or so single engine enemy aircraft were sighted approaching from the land. This came to nothing as far as Eric was concerned. All the while heavy and accurate anti-aircraft fire was rising into the sky from shore batteries although no aircraft were damaged. Flying in NV-O, the pilot states seeing two enemy aircraft attacking Eric and a third attacking another Beaufighter. One of the fighter escort Beaufighters left his formation to act as a decoy and was seen heading in land with five 109s on his tail. Neither Eric nor the pilot of NV-O sighted any shipping and neither suffered any damage. After refuelling at Wick, he returned to base landing 2224hrs. The last two entries in Eric's logbook record him doing night flying training and a night cross country flight. Unfortunately, he did not keep his logbook up to date from this point with no account of any flying he undertook. Because of this omission it is not possible to trace Eric's own flight to North Africa. The following information is obtained from other sources.

Towards the end of May having converted from the Beaufighter Mk VI to the torpedo carrying TF MK X (which was also armed with cannon) the Squadron departed for North Africa. The conversion from one to the other consisted of collecting the new aircraft from Bristol's factory at Filton and carrying out several test flights in preparation for the journey ahead. The most important test was fuel consumption! Sixteen aircraft left Tain airfield bound for Portreath in Cornwall, for a stopover. From here they left for Gibraltar and then on to North Africa. Two aircraft were lost on the way, with fourteen landing at Protville II just to the south of Tunis. I have been able to establish the exact reason behind the losses, but it was probably due to engine failure or other problems with the aircraft. This represented about 10% of the flight lost. The remaining crews and ground crew went by sea to Algiers and then on to Bilda. The final part of the journey was made by road. Following the working up period and familiarisation the Squadron became operational in June.

(Author' Note; An interesting entry in Eric's brother Stanley's logbook shows that he had also arrived at Protville II on 10th June 1943. 39 Squadron was converting to the Beaufighter TF Mk X. On the 19th Stanley was taken up in Beaufighter JM387, piloted by Eric, it would have been interesting to have both accounts of this).

The nature of operations over the Mediterranean was low level in order to keep below the enemy radar height. One major difficulty this presented was the fact that the Mediterranean was normally a flat sea whereas the North Sea was rough. This meant that it was far more difficult to judge the height above sea level. When flying at only 50ft above the sea such a calculation was critical. The Squadron's first mission in North Africa, on 22nd June was a disaster. Eric was tasked with leading a recon-naissance/strike, taking off at 1624 in Beaufighter NV-D with his navigator, Flight Sergeant Ernest William Alexander. Less than an hour into the mission at 1715

South east of Sardinia off Cagliari his aircraft was seen to pull up suddenly from the height of fifty feet above sea level and dive nose first into the water. One member of the crew was seen to have escaped the wreckage and to be clinging to the dinghy that had not fully inflated. This was recognised as Eric.

The other three aircraft circled the wreckage and the pilot of K, Flying Officer R.A. Johnson, and his navigator Sergeant M Potts, sent an S.O.S message to raise the alarm. This action resulted in Air Sea Rescue being launched. Flying Officer Johnson jettisoned his torpedo in preparation to drop their dinghy. As the dinghy was being dropped K collided with N causing damage to the starboard tailplane, ripping off the elevator and damaging the rudder trimming bar on K, and N the starboard propeller was damaged causing severe vibration. The two aircraft set course for base. Sergeant Murray in P followed, fearing the other two might not get back. As the aircraft left the scene Eric was seen waving cheerily to his comrades. On arrival at base K and N crash landed with no injuries to either crew.

Although Eric had been seen to escape the aircraft no sign of him was ever seen again. Although the weather was fine, visibility was 15-20 miles and the sea was calm, the air-sea rescue effort failed to find him. Aircraft taking part in this search were Wellingtons, Baltimores and Beaufighters. The crews of the other three aircraft were Flying Officer R A Johnson and Sergeant Potts in NV- K, Flying Officer J W King and Flight Sergeant J D M Harvie in NV-N and Sergeant's J M Murray and L Rice in P. It is not clear what happened to cause the accident. Eric aged 26 and his navigator were posted missing on 22nd June 1943. A letter sent to Daisy, from the adjutant of 144 squadron, dated 1st July gives scant details about what happened. The letter does go on to say that some of Eric's personal effects had been passed to Stanley who was on

Letter concerning the loss of Eric

the same airfield. There is also high praise for Eric, he was always keen and willing to get on with the job in hand and make sure it was completed. He was regarded as one of the best pilots on 144 Squadron.

Eric and Ernest Alexander are both commemorated on the Malta War Memorial. Eric on Panel 6 Column 2 and Ernest on Panel 7 Column 1.

Eric did not live to achieve his full potential in the RAF. He was one of the 83% of Torpedo Bomber crews that were killed before completing their first tour of operations. It was a highly stressful job for the crews flying at extremely low level over the sea. In addition to facing the danger of incoming anti-aircraft fire there was the risk that the ship you were attacking might explode and take the aircraft out of the sky. Later in the war this became a hazard for many crews operating over land and shooting up locomotives, as was the case for Stuart in Burma. Many aircraft received damage from this alone, regardless of enemy action. When Eric crashed, the crews of all the squadrons operating in and around the Mediterranean were hard pushed. It was of vital importance to deny the enemy his supplies. Reading Eric's logbook, the comments made about him suggest that he may have made a higher rank had he survived.

CHAPTER 4

Stanley Muller-Rowland

Squadron Leader 103498, Stanley Muller-Rowland DFC and Bar was one of twins, his brother being Stuart, born in 1920.

Initially educated at Sunnydown, Hogs back, Guildford, Surrey from November 1933 to July 1935, Stanley and John followed their brother Eric to Uppingham School. The two boys boarded in West Bank House as did Eric. They both started at Uppingham in September 1935 and in 1937 Stanley achieved credits in Scripture Knowledge, English, History, French (both written and oral), Physics and Chemistry. Stanley left Uppingham in December 1938 and Stuart left the following March. An out-going lad, Stanley, enjoyed life, unlike his twin who was quieter and much more reserved. While at Uppingham, Stanley was in the Officer Cadet Training Corps, achieving the rank of Sergeant.

Stanley in Rugby kit. Photograph by permission of Uppingham School

On leaving school Stanley was not able to follow his brother Eric into the business as a corn merchant, who, as eldest son had accepted the duty of following his father. Instead, Stanley chose to become a shipping clerk, which related well as the business involved the shipping of corn.

Stanley along with his brother Stuart enlisted in the Royal Air Force on 29th July 1940 at 2 Recruits Centre (RC), R.A.F Cardington, Bedfordshire as AC 2 1183360. Stanley's home address was given as Purford Woods, Purford, Surrey. His description was given as 5ft 7ins in height, dark brown hair, grey eyes, a fair complexion, and moles on his left cheek.

Stanley moved to 9 RC on 10th of August, followed by a move to St Athan, Wales on 28th August, with the initial grading of Aircraft Hand/Pilot. On 28th September he joined No1 Reserve Command, 3 Initial Training Wing to complete his basic training. This basic training applied to all new recruits in the RAF, introducing them to service life, drill, and discipline, as well as ground instruction on the elementary aspects of navigation, signals, and gunnery. Once this

The twins in flying gear (Stuart on right, Stanley on left)

The twins in uniform (Stuart on left, Stanley on right)

process was complete, he was accepted as a pilot under training on 14th December. This was to be done in Rhodesia (now Zimbabwe).

Stanley reported for flying training on 8th January the following year. Under the British Commonwealth Air

Training Plan, flying training was taking place throughout the Commonwealth. Stanley went to No 27 E.F.T.S. Induna, Bulawayo, Rhodesia, making his first flight in D H Tiger Moth R4816 with Flying Officer Dawlish at the controls. Stanley was promoted to Sergeant on 2nd April. On passing out he was classed as above average with a mark of 90.6.

Stanley moved on to 21 S.F.T.S at Kumalo, Bulawayo on 2nd April 1941 to carry out his conversion and training on multi engine aircraft. He was flying Air Speed Oxfords and passed out with a mark of 84.7%. On 17th May Stanley was certified competent to act as a safety pilot and awarded his wings on the 20th. The job of a safety pilot was to fly with other students so that if they encountered difficulties the safety pilot could step in and take control.

Once his training was completed in Rhodesia, Stanley was discharged from the RAF on 8th July and accepted into the RAFVR as a probationary Pilot Officer on a short service commission with the new service number of 103498. His commission was listed in the London Gazette on 12th September. On his new service record his mother Daisy now of Grass Stones, Sea Way, Middleton on Sea, Sussex was stated as his next of kin.

Stanley's next posting was to the Advanced Training School with the S.F.T.S. This involved photo reconnaissance, low, medium, and high-level bombing practice and numerous night and day cross country flights with Stanley flying as safety pilot on many of these exercises. He left here with an average grading.

At the end of June Stanley moved on to No 61 Air School, School of General Reconnaissance, to learn various search and reconnaissance techniques. Stanley converted onto the other twin-engine aircraft used mainly for training purposes which included the Avro

Anson, a solid robust aircraft, well suited for the type of training he was to carry out. The course ended on 10th October. Stanley's time in Rhodesia was now finished.

Stanley was to realise his forte in his next posting, this was to No 5 OTU at Chivenor, North Devon. Joining the course in January 1942, Stanley had his first Air Experience flight in the Bristol Beaufort on the 30th with Squadron Leader Simmons at the controls. He was flying solo on the aircraft by 17th February.

Most of February was spent getting used to this aircraft which was quite different to any that he had flown previously. The OTU had the bomber variant of the Avro Anson on charge and it in this that Stanley flew on his first bombing practice where he carried out several exercises, including dropping a stick of bombs from 600ft. Initially bombing static objects Stanley then progressed to attacking moving targets. It was here that he met his crew of Sergeants Anderson, Friend and Gillespie.

Night flying appeared as a regular exercise with Stanley adapting well to this. The next thing that he had to learn was dive bombing, which was the type of bombing that Stanley excelled at. Other aspects of his training included the use of depth charges and air-to-air and air-to-surface firing

Stanley in uniform

using the cannons. On completion of the course Stanley had achieved a mark of 79.5% and the assessment was: "Good dive bombing and very good flying for low level crew bombing".

A posting to No1 Ferry Training unit at RAF Lyneham was the next step for Stanley. Travelling to Filton, Bristol, Stanley collected a new Beaufort (DD975) from the Bristol Aircraft Factory and flew back to Lyneham on 2nd May. The 3rd, 4th and 5th were spent doing air tests and preparing the aircraft for its long flight on 9th when Stanley and his crew left Lyneham for Porteath, Cornwall. They stopped over at Porteath until the 13th. With the aircraft fully fuelled Stanley was on his way to Gibraltar. He stopped here to check over the aircraft and refuel, before leaving on 17th for the flight on to Malta – another stopover – before finally flying to 108 MU on 19th May. 108 MU was located at LG222 Kilo 17 on the Cairo to Fayoum Road, Egypt. As this was a ferry flight Stanley returned to No5 (C) O.T.U. on a returning transport aircraft.

It appears that Stanley did not fly again until 20th August when he carried out a series of night flying tests for the remainder of the month. September was taken up with a mixture of bombing practices from varying heights against fixed and moving targets. Air-to-air and air-to-sea firing came into this training period. On the 21st Stanley had a flight in a Bristol Blenheim for air experience, the next month he flew the Blenheim on several occasions. This was a gunnery course for the crew, a concentrated period of air to air and air to sea firing and using the camera gun.

Stanley piloted three air gunners and his navigator on these flights in Avro Ansons, Blenheims and Hampdens. The gunners were all gaining the valuable experience that, in the future, might well save their lives and those of their fellow crew members. Stanley was obviously a very capable pilot by now, as on 2nd of October he was gaining air experience in a Westland Lysander and on the 5th, he was towing the drogue target with it. This experience was to stand him in good stead for his next posting. For the second time Stanley flew to Filton, Bristol to collect a new Beaufort DW880, taking this to Lyneham with his crew of Sergeants Anderson, Gillespie and Friend.

On the 31st they carried out an anti-surface vessel test, the Beaufort was now being fitted with the new air-surface vessel radar. Returning to Lyneham before flying on to Portreath for the journey to Malta via Gibraltar, he landed on 2nd November at Luqa, Malta. Stanley took an older Beaufort L9802, from Luqa to Safi, as his aircraft had been damaged on landing.

Malta, in the earlier part of the war had suffered badly from the attention of the Italian and German air forces. For the valiant defence shown by the Island as a whole King George awarded the George Cross to the Island on 15th April 1942, this being the first for a collective award of the Cross, the only other occasions being to the Royal Ulster Constabulary on 23rd November 1999 and to the National Health Service on 5th July 2021. Malta was strategically important both to the British for the operations in the Mediterranean and to the Axis forces for the resupply of equipment to its troops in North Africa: the former as it was a major harbour for the Royal Navy and the latter due to convoys being harried by the Royal Navy and RAF. Once the RAF started to gain air superiority more aircraft could be based there to assist in the disruption of the German convoys bound for North Africa.

For seven months in 1941 the aircraft based on Malta accounted for 56% of the Axis merchant shipping being sunk. Even though the Axis forces had taken over several French ships and the Italian shipyards were building to capacity this loss rate was totally unsustainable. With losses running at that rate Rommel's Afrika Korps would not last a year. As the Allied air power grew so did the losses to the Axis shipping. To quote from Pierre Clostermann's book "Flames in the Sky":

> *Malta, a small island with an area of about*
> *90 square miles, isolated by the fall of France*
> *in 1940 and the lack of vision by the military*
> *chiefs in North Africa, was a thorn in the flesh*
> *of the Axis powers. That thorn produced a*
> *malignant abscess and the Afrika Korps, in*
> *spite of the genius of Rommel, died of it.*

Pierre Clostermann, Legion d'Honneur, DFC and Bar.

Stanley was posted to 39 Squadron, a mixed unit, with South Africans, Australians, Canadians, New Zealanders, and British. Life was now going to get busy for Stanley. On 12th November 1942 he took off for a mine laying mission to the harbour at Tunis but due to bad weather the target could not be located. On the 22nd he went on a bombing raid to Linosa and on the 24th and 27th was mine laying at Bizerta. With Stanley flying AW284, the harbour at Palermo, Sicily was the target for the 29th. Stanley notes that Flight Sergeant E Walker and his crew of Sergeant R J McCulloch, Sergeant D Stevens and Sergeant G R A Duffield were missing after this mission, no mention is made of what happened to them. A slight change came in December when on the 7th, 10th, and 22nd, Stanley was going on anti-submarine patrols off Malta to protect a convoy of ships carrying supplies to the beleaguered island.

Conditions in Malta when Stanley arrived were primitive. The Island had suffered heavy bombings from the

German and Italian air forces based in Sicily. Fresh water and food were scarce: pilots could not get enough water to wash in, what was available was for cooking and drinking. The ground and aircrews were wearing not much more than rags, their uniforms being worn out and there were no replacements.

Men were living in tunnels, either in the hillsides or constructed as shelters. Stanley's arrival in Malta coincided with what was known as the November Convoy that signalled the end of the Siege of Malta. The convoy brought in food supplies to bolster the near starvation diet. One report states that lunch consisted of five shrivelled olives, one slice of fried corned beef, four ounces of bread and three semi-ripe figs, all washed down with one cup of tea. The pilots had the extra "ration" of two tablespoons of shredded carrot soaked in olive oil and a sulphur pill to fend off diarrhoea. If the men smelt oil burning near the cook house at any time this often meant that lunch might be soup. The oil used for cooking was used engine oil from the aircraft, as there was no coal and the smell permeated everywhere.

The vegetables on the island were not particularly good, as many servicemen, tired and worn out succumbed to "Malta Dog", a type of dysentery. It was not just the servicemen that suffered these conditions, and it was not just for the duration of the war. The civilian population also endured hardships while the infant mortality rate rose, and the effects of malnourishment left lasting effects on many.

Authors note; In the coming paragraphs "Rover" and "Strike" are used. A "Rover" is a formation of four or eight aircraft going out to look for targets of opportunity and a "Strike" is a planned attack on a known target based on intelligence gathered by a reconnaissance patrol. A reconnaissance patrol was launched with the sole intention of gathering information and avoiding getting involved in a fight with the enemy. It would be pointless should the aircraft get shot down without the information gathered not getting back to base. The term used for mine laying operations was "gardening", planting their "vegetables" – mines.

Stanley undertook three anti-submarine patrols in December, all carried out in front of friendly convoys and all without incident. In November nineteen German submarines had slipped past the defenders on Gibraltar into the Mediterranean. These had already sunk some Royal Navy vessels and threatened the supply convoys to and from Malta. To try to overcome this a greater emphasis was placed on convoy protection. With re-organisation in the Squadron, leave was granted in mid-December. The personnel spent their leave in Egypt. It was a welcome break. It appears that all had the opportunity to enjoy a better quality of beer, than was available in Malta, where what beer was available was watered down. Egypt offered many distractions for the visitors from Malta. Getting away from the air raids they could relax for a while. Stanley with his sense of fun enjoyed this.

On 12th January, Stanley along with three other aircraft flew a mine laying mission off Melita Island. With Lt Lore flying a DC3, Stanley left Malta for No 5 Middle East Torpedo School (METS) at LG 224, RAF Shallufa on 15th January 1943. It was here that he and his crew were to hone their skills in the use of torpedoes. With the course ending on 8th February Stanley had completed 25hrs 55mins daytime flying and 6hrs 30mins night flying and was assessed as "Good Average".

Leaving Shallufa on the 9th, Stanley and his crew made their way back to Malta via Berga III, Libya. On the 14th, 17th and 19th February Stanley took part in "Torpedo

Rover" attacks to Marsala-Palermo and Maritimo-Palermo-Carbonara, but with no targets sighted they returned to base on all three days. Rommel's fuel supplies were his target. The tanker *Thorsheimer*, a Norwegian vessel that had been requisitioned from Norway, had delivered 10,000 tons of fuel to Bizerta in January. The British reconnaissance flights had seen the whereabouts of the tanker and intelligence reports stated that it was leaving Naples early on 20th February. The following day a further attack was made with no results. In the afternoon, a force of B25 Mitchell bombers of the USAAF bombed the convoy and two bombs hit *Thorsheimer* but one failed to explode. Although Stanley did not take part, the final attack was made on the 23rd by which time the tender vessels had evacuated the crew. Six aircraft from 39 Squadron were sent to finish her off, this they did in style, with four torpedoes dropped and all four-hitting home – the *Thorsheimer* sank shortly after.

Stanley's luck continued when, on 20th February, he attacked a tanker, one motor vessel (M/V) and two torpedo boats near Palermo. No hits were observed on the tanker, but it was sunk the following day by Captain Tilley of the South African Air Force, with Flight Sergeant Deacon and Flying Officer Feast. Another visit to Maritimo-Palermo on the 23rd resulted in an attack on a destroyer with no results observed followed by an attack with machine guns on a small M/V. The 25th saw Stanley and his crew making a strike on one cruiser, two destroyers and two motor vessels 100 miles North of Maritimo. One of the M/Vs, a vessel of 6-7000 tons, was hit amidships and sank five minutes later, following a hit by the torpedo of Flying Officer Cartwright. Two days later the Maritimo-Palermo areas were targeted again although Stanley lists no results for this attack.

On 4th March Stanley was promoted to Flight Lieutenant.

Operations for March opened for Stanley with a night flare attack on the 8th on Cleopatra, (this appears in Stanley's logbook, but I am not sure what this is supposed to mean, possibly a code name?). A strike on two M/Vs and three destroyers near C.Stilo was called off when the aircraft had to return to base. A daylight raid on Cleopatra on the 12th was the first of two raids that day, the second being a 'Torpedo Rover' when the squadron sighted and attacked a tanker of 10,000 tons, with one M/V and five destroyers, a least one hit was observed on the tanker with clouds of smoke being emitted. With a fighter escort of Beaufighters from 273 Squadron, 17th March was a day with some good results when Stanley was part of a daylight strike on one 10,000 ton tanker which was disguised as an M/V and two destroyer escorts 90 miles off C.Stilo. His own torpedo dropped and ran straight. A total of eight torpedoes were dropped by the various aircraft, three of which were seen to find their targets and the tanker was sunk. Me110s were operating over the ships as cover for them. It is noted in Stanley's log-book that there were at least seven Me110s with more enemy aircraft seen in the distance. Stanley's gunner fired and claimed one as a probable and his Wireless Operator/Air Gunner (Wop/Ag) claimed one as 'damaged'. The final tally was one destroyed, four 'damaged' and two 'probables'. A later "Rover" on Maritimo-Palermo-Carbonara proved to be a fruitless mission with no sightings being made. March ended with Stanley flying 14hrs 45mins operational, giving him a total of 120 operational hours.

On 29th March "The Times of Malta" ran the list of awards announced by HQ Malta Air Command. These included Wing Commander Maurice Larwood-Gaine AFC (39 Squadron) being awarded the DSO. A bar to the DFC for Major Donald Pax Tilley (39 Squadron) of the South African Air Force with DFC's being awarded to Squadron

Leader George Byrne Stanislaus Coleman, Squadron Leader Norman John Starr, Flight Lieutenant Stanley Rowland Muller-Rowland, *(39 Squadron), Flying Officer Peter William Stokes and Pilot Officer Ewan Gillies (39 Squadron). On Stanley's service record this is listed as the 9th of April. The citation in the London Gazette dated 9th April 1943 reads:

> *Acting Flight Lieutenant Stanley Muller-Rowland, RAFVR. 39 Squadron. This officer has taken part in 22 operational missions, involving attacks on shipping, minelaying missions and bombing sorties. In February 1943 he flew one aircraft of a formation which attacked a supply ship escorted by four destroyers. Hits were obtained, one of them by Flight Lieutenant Muller-Rowland who released a torpedo which struck the supply vessel amid-ships. In March 1943 he took part in another successful attack on a merchant ship. Some days later he participated in a daylight attack on a convoy of one tanker and three destroyers heavily escorted by fighters. In spite of the formidable opposition, Flight Lieutenant Muller-Rowland released his torpedo with accuracy. This officer has displayed great skill and courage, pressing home his attacks with vigour.*

The raids mentioned above were reported in the Times of Malta, on 26th February 1943. Stanley, obviously proud of the citation, sent the newspaper cutting home to his mother Daisy who, equally proud, stuck these in her scrap book.

---

* This is Stanley's full name. Each of the brothers had 'Rowland' as a middle name.

In much the same way April continued with more strikes on enemy shipping. Although Stanley was not involved, on the 10th and 11th the Squadron lost two aircraft. After the first loss, a Beaufort took off on the 11th at first light to conduct a search for dinghies with no luck. Later on that day an aircraft on patrol was attacked and shot down by night fighters. As a result of an international broadcast by an enemy aircraft on the 17th an amphibious Air Sea Rescue Supermarine Walrus was launched and successfully rescued one of the two crews.

(Authors note; a radio message could be passed on an open frequency which could be picked up by anyone. These broadcasts were sent in plain language rather than in cypher).

The first mission for Stanley was on 12th April, when he undertook a First Light and Sunrise patrol on Orion and Cleopatra. On the 15th he went on a dawn patrol to the Sicilian Channel and dropped his torpedo on a ship of 3-4000 tons although no hits were observed. On the 23rd he was airborne again when he carried out a strike on one M/V of 12000 tons North of Maritimo. Dropping his torpedo at 2145hrs the ship was struck amidships causing an explosion and sending smoke and flashes high into the sky. Observing from a distance he sent a signal to the other aircraft and sent them in to finish the ship off. She finally sank within five minutes following a hit from another aircraft. April proved a successful month for the squadron.

On 6th May the Squadron planned to set out on a mine laying operation to Trapini harbour. This was not carried out as no diversionary operation had been put in place so it was deemed too much of a risk with enemy aircraft operating in the area and the Beauforts would have been sitting targets. By nature of the operation, the Beauforts had to fly low and steady at a lower speed than normal. A change of operations occurred on the 10th when the

Squadron made a "Bombing Rover" to Southern Sicily, where Stanley dropped 4x250lb bombs on Marsala from a height of 7500ft. Four aircraft took off, one returned early due to engine failure and another one failed to locate the target Stanley and Sergeant Finn intended to attack. The Beauforts were getting war weary due to the lack of spares coupled with the fact that the Bristol Taurus engine struggled to cope in the climate. Arriving over the centre of town Stanley went in first and successfully bombed but Sergeant Finn's bombs failed to release. Finn made two runs and on both the bombs still failed to release. The result was that only one of the four aircraft that took off successfully bombed the target.

On the 11th May a 4000-ton M/V was attacked with no results observed. A strike on the 18th, on a 10000-ton tanker left it beached with no further result. Stanley had made two dummy runs on the tanker to get himself into the best possible position to attack. Apart from the beaching, which was seen by reconnaissance the next day, Stanley could see no more as the tanker had put up a smoke screen. Stanley's aircraft Beaufort DD904 was damaged by A/A fire which burst the tail wheel tyre and holed the elevator. This was to be the last operation that Stanley flew from Malta.

After only two months as Flight Lieutenant, Stanley was promoted to Squadron Leader on 18th May. Lee Heide states in his book "Whispering Death" that out of the eighteen crews in the Squadron when he arrived on 3rd July 1942, only three were left, these being Stanley, Major Don Tilley, SAAF and Paddy Garland, RCAF. No crews had managed to complete a tour in the Squadron during that time. Many had come and gone for various reasons, not all because of enemy action. Some crew members had been posted to training units on receiving promotion and others had been posted to other squadrons to build up the numbers of experienced crews.

Leaving Malta on 1st June, Stanley took extra passengers to North Africa. Life in North Africa was harsh, conditions were primitive. The accommodation for all ranks was tented. On some airfields shanty towns sprang up, the buildings consisting of empty petrol cans, packing cases and tent canvas. The ground and aircrews lived in these structures. At Stanley's airfield the aircrews had arrived before the ground crews, so nothing had been prepared, as was so often the case. There were no tents, so the crews spent the first couple of nights sleeping underneath their aircraft.

The airfield itself was no more than compressed sand which in times of heavy rain would turn to a muddy strip. It did not often rain, but when it did it would make the airfield extremely difficult to operate from. Furthermore, when it rained, water would occasionally run like a river through the tents. When it was dry, and the wind got up, it carried sand into the tents so the kit of the airmen was always covered in sand. The heat during the day was sometimes too much to bear and the nights could get very cold. For the ground crews conditions were even worse, as they had to repair, re-arm and refuel the aircraft with no protection from the elements. During the day, the temperatures would get so high that to touch the flat sides of the aircraft would inevitably cause burning. The heat caused tyres to burst and fuel lines to leak, raising the risk that aircraft might catch fire in flight.

As several operations were carried out by night and with the makeshift nature of many of the landing strips there was no proper provision for flare paths. This was overcome by taking the top off petrol cans, filling them with sand, pouring petrol on the sand and setting light to it. (*Authors note, with the price of petrol at the time of writing, 2020, it would be un-thinkable now*). This would give the pilots a straight line to follow when taking off and landing. Flying around various bases there Stanley was to end up at Protville II, to the south of Tunis, arriving on 18th June. It was here that the 39 Squadron was to re-equip with the Bristol Beaufighter.

An interesting entry appears in Stanley's logbook for 19th June 1943. Flying in Bristol Beaufighter JM387 the pilot is identified as Flying Officer Eric Muller-Rowland and Stanley as passenger on a demonstration flight. This came about because 39 Squadron had moved to Portville II alongside 47 and 144 Squadrons that formed 328 Wing. 39 was converting to the Beaufighter from the Bristol Beaufort. Eric, Stanley's brother was with 144 Squadron which was already equipped with Beaufighters. This incident occurred three days before Eric was killed. Unfortunately, Eric had not kept up his logbook since 3rd May so this does not appear as it would have been an interesting addition to have the entry of self (Eric) as pilot and passenger Squadron Leader Muller-Rowland (Stanley). Later, on the 19th, flying in Beaufighter JM387, Stanley gained experience on the type in preparation for further training for himself and to train other pilots for the remainder of June.

It must have been a huge shock for Stanley on the 22nd when news arrived at base that his brother Eric had been killed working out of the same airfield. This must have been compounded by the fact that only three days before they had flown together.

When the Axis forces left Tunisia, they left behind a vast amount of equipment on the coast. A group from the Squadron went off to look at this. Two of the number were Stanley and Lee Heide. The Germans had made a good job of destroying things so that they could not be used but two things they had not destroyed were a Volkswagen and a large Mercedes staff car. One of the other sightseers helped himself to the Volkswagen which was to become the unofficial Squadron transport and Stanley and Lee took the Mercedes.

With General Erwin Rommel's Afrika Corps being dislodged from North Africa his supply lines from Italy were of vital importance to him. The Royal Air Force, along with units of the South African, Australian, and Free French air forces, caused major disruption round the coast of Italy. Allied to this was the impending invasion of Sicily, with units of these air forces softening up the port defences in preparation.

The invasion of Sicily took place on 10th July. All the Beaufighter Squadrons became involved in convoy protection or attacking enemy positions. Covering the invasion ports was always a huge risk for the pilots as the Royal Navy tended to shoot first and worry about consequences later. The anti-shipping role continued alongside these operations to disrupt the enemy's supplies.

Stanley's first operation on the new aircraft was on 11th July in LX793 when the target was 90 miles Southbound from Naples. The pilots sighted an M/V of 4-5000 tons with two destroyers and one flak ship. Dropping his torpedo, the M/V was hit on the bows leaving them crumpled. One of the destroyers was also damaged. Three aircraft were hit by fighters off Sicily with one being shot down. Stanley's LX793 was hit by A/A fire and damaged. This proved to be a poor start for Stanley and his navigator, Flying Officer Anderson, as Stanley crashed on landing back at base. As strike leader on the 14th, Stanley, in the rapidly repaired LX793, led the formation to a position 220 miles northeast of Monte Cristo. Here they attacked and sunk a tanker of 5000 tons which blew up. A second tanker of 1500 tons was left burning. The tanker was protected by three flak ships one of which was sunk by cannon fire from the guns of Pilot Officer Leam Garlands aircraft. Stanley dropped his torpedo late and did not observe any hit. The danger with attacking tankers was that when they were hit, they did sometimes blow up, resulting in debris being thrown high into the air. Many a time aircraft flew through this debris because they had no time to take evasive action. Several aircraft suffered damage and worse through this.

Stanley was earning himself a reputation for teaching other aircrew. He would often take out newly posted pilots to demonstrate or teach them new skills and assess their ability as pilots and leaders. When not on operations much of his time was taken up with this. This was later demonstrated in his next posting. As torpedo strike leader, on the 21st, Stanley led a formation to attack a convoy of two M/V's and five escort vessels (E/V). Ten miles off Bastia the aircraft struck. No results were observed from the strike, but the formation received a fair amount of anti-aircraft fire from the E/V's. The next strike as leader was to have much better results. On the 30th, with a mixture of cannon fire and torpedoes the formation left behind a scene of devastation with one M/V sunk by two torpedo strikes. This vessel was on tow following a previous attack by a torpedo dropped by an aircraft of 47 Squadron; another ship was hit amidships by a torpedo and one more severely damaged by cannon fire.

During August Stanley only took part in one strike, this was to Naples Bay on the 16th when the formation attacked a small convoy. The convoy comprised two MV's, one of 4000 tons and the other of 3500 tons, three escort destroyers and a Junkers JU 88 flying as top cover. The two MV's and one destroyer were left smoking. Stanley's aircraft was damaged by anti-aircraft fire from the E/V although he managed to return to base. Also, on this strike, the aircraft of Flying Officer G L May and Sergeant Baker was badly shot up. Flying Officer May almost made it back to base but crashed just before landing. Neither of the crew were injured. The remainder of the month was taken up with demonstrations and training for new aircrew, practicing formation flying and cannon practice.

On 24th August it was announced that Stanley had been awarded a Bar to his DFC. In the Supplement of the London Gazette dated 24th August 1943 his citation reads; Squadron Leader Stanley Muller-Rowland, RAFVR, 39 Squadron.

> *"This officer is a highly efficient flight commander whose continuous good work has been worthy of great praise. In July 1943 he led a section of torpedo carrying aircraft on an attack on a medium sized supply ship and its escort vessel. In spite of fighter opposition hits were obtained on both vessels. Three days later Squadron Leader Muller-Rowland led another formation in an attack against a tanker escorted by three ships and with fighter cover. Despite the opposition the tanker was destroyed while one escort vessel was set on fire. On both occasions Squadron Leader Muller-Rowland displayed faultless leadership and great determination".*

September was to prove a busy time for Stanley, starting with a fighter affiliation exercise in Beaufighter JL530 with Pilot Officer Cecil Leroy "Lee" Heide, a Canadian, on the 6th. With Pilot Officer "Paddy" Garland flying in another Beaufighter, Stanley carried out a number of simulated attacks on him, and then reversed the roles with Paddy making the attacks. Lee gave Stanley orders from his navigator's position as to where Paddy was.

As Stanley took violent evasive action, the starboard engine seized, the cylinder head was blown off No 4-cylinder taking with it the engine cowling and the propeller flew over the Perspex canopy of the navigator's position. The instruments did not give any indication of a problem before the engine seized, although there appears to have been a complete loss of oil. Going into a spiral dive Stanley fought the controls to get out of situation. He finally regained control of the aircraft at about 1500ft. Looking for a suitable place to make a crash landing he found a ploughed field. Bouncing once, the aircraft ploughed across the field and came to a stop just before it toppled into a drainage ditch. Other than a sore back Lee Heide had no injuries and Stanley got a severe bruise on his forehead from hitting the gunsight that he had obviously not had time to stow before the crash.

(Foot note; there is a small confusion over which engine seized. In Stanley's logbook he says it was the starboard engine whereas Lee Heide says it was the port engine in his book).

Flying overhead, Paddy Garland gave a running commentary to base. The crew retrieved the essential pieces from the aircraft. Not so long after coming down the two were picked up and returned to base with the Beaufighter being recovered a few days later. On the 7th as strike leader again, Stanley led a formation to carry out a torpedo and cannon rover, to cover an area from the East Coast of Corsica – Leghorn and the West Coast of Corsica. Approximately 20 miles West of Rousse Island they spotted a motor vessel of about 2500 tons. An extraordinarily successful attack was made with torpedoes and cannon sinking the ship. During the attack Swiss markings were seen on the vessel. I have found no explanation for this. It might well have been a case of mistaken identification or misreporting.

Stanley's last offensive operation with 39 Squadron was a strike on a convoy ten miles to the north of Elba. They attacked a tanker and four E/Vs on the 15th, but no results were observed. Two crews were lost on this mission, these being Flying Officers J C Yorke and W B Mathias in Q JM386 and Flying Officers M D Cox and W Speary in NJM387. Another aircraft LX785 flown by Flying Officer Ambrose and his navigator Flying Officer G J Higgin was badly shot up. Ambrose managed to ditch successfully in the sea about twenty miles from Cape Carbonara. Flight Lieutenant Butler with his navigator were sent out to search the area soon after the report was received but found nothing.

The following day three aircraft were sent out to continue the search, Stanley was flying on one of these with Flight Sergeant Anderson. All three crews located the dinghies and after they had reported the position circled once over them. An air sea rescue was sent out along with a Supermarine Walrus ASR aircraft. Stanley was able to assist the ASR launch to home in on the position so enabling the two occupants of the dinghies to be rescued 24 hours after ditching. It was noted that towards the end of his tour, Stanley was starting to show signs of strain. After taking part in so many operations and with the death of Eric on his mind it is no wonder. The blow of Eric's death had been compounded by the fact they were co-located on the same airfield. After completing his last mission with 39, a group drove (in the trusty re-allocated VW) into Tunis for Stanley's farewell party. The venue was a night club, the Restaurant de Bluet. Staying open until the early hours of the morning with belly dancers and music for entertainment, the airmen ended the party with the Squadron song.

> "When you hear the news that a ship has been sunk,
> That another Jerry cruiser is just a heap of junk,
> Then you know that the boys are going to get drunk.

That's good old 39
Torping shipping.
Everybody thinks it's awfully ripping.
Look out for that mast!
Or it might be your last.

Leaving the night club, they found that someone had stolen their car. It was to show up a couple of days later when it was spotted outside the 47 Squadron HQ. It did not stay there long!

While serving as a Flight Lieutenant with 39 Squadron Stanley was noted as being very charismatic, with a ready smile and someone who lived life to the full. Although quietly spoken with a slight build he was respected by the men under his command as well as those officers senior to him. Stanley was noted for his prowess. He could handle an aircraft easily with an almost natural ability. In the mess he would be one of the boys, taking part in the fun and games. This last comment relates back to his days at home when he was known as the "Wizard of Woking". In contrast he would take his role seriously. A born leader, he was a natural when it came to combat and showed no fear. Always eager to take part in operations, Stanley showed a disregard of danger and was willing to take risks – it was a rare quality. This was not his only strength; he was always trying to assess the tactics used and looking at ways to improve methods of attacking the enemy. He was worth the esteem he was held in by other members of the Squadron who treated him with the highest regard as did several senior officers.

On completion of his tour of operations, a posting to 5 Middle East Torpedo School (METS) followed Stanley's time on 39 Squadron. Stanley's first few days at 5 M.E.T.S. were spent flying passengers to various airfields in the area. This was in a variety of, by now war weary, Beaufort MkIs and II's. Operationally the time at 5 M.E.T.S was not terribly exciting. The job was to train and select new leaders for posting out to squadrons or giving refresher courses to other experienced crews. An emphasis was put on night attacks using torpedoes with the Royal Navy providing ships as targets for the dummy torpedoes, usually carried out on a moonlit night or on a moonless night the targets would be illuminated by flares dropped near the ship by a Wellington bomber.

An opportunity arose for Stanley to get his hands on something quite different in the form of an obsolete Fairey Gordon on the 7th. Another task was ferrying senior officers around. The closest to operational flying came on the 16th when Stanley flew over a crashed aircraft so it could be found by a rescue party and on the 25th when he took part in a search for the dinghies of some downed aircrew, he does not say where in his logbook.

November was to be much the same with ferry flights and training. On the 13th several experienced pilots and crews along with some selected crews who had just recently been trained were needed to bolster numbers on various squadrons on a temporary basis. Boarding a DC3 Stanley and twelve others re-located from Shallufa to El Adem via Gambut. Stanley was temporarily attached to 603 Squadron. Later the same day, in an operation consisting of 603 and 47 Squadrons and taking off at 1300, Stanley, flying Beaufighter X LX928 KU-D, a 47 Squadron aircraft, led a formation of nine Beaufighters on an offensive sweep round Leros. In company with two Mitchell B25 bombers from the USAAF, the formation passed through the Kaso strait towards Leros. The sweep proved to be uneventful, so the flight turned for base.

STANLEY MULLER-ROWLAND

On their return they encountered enemy. The formation attacked twelve Junkers JU88s three of which were damaged. Stanley's aircraft received hits from the return fire and with both engines being knocked out and the starboard engine on fire he was forced to ditch in the sea north of Patmos. Stanley and his navigator, Pilot Officer Anderson, were seen to escape from the aircraft and climb into their dinghies. Stanley was posted missing according to his service record. Although they were both wounded, they were rescued by a Greek fishing boat. Moving from island to island they eventually reached Turkey on 24th of November when word got back to 5 METS that both were safe and well. Travelling through Syria and Palestine they went back to Egypt where they returned to Shallufa on the 26th, returning to flying on the 27th in non-operational roles until 5th December.

Authors note. Stanley uses his "attachment to 603" as a slightly tongue in cheek comment, this was from 1200 to 1600hrs on the 13th. (The dates above are from Squadron records and I have chosen to leave them in although they do not tally up with the telegrams).

On 20th November 1943, Flight Lieutenant Smith, adjutant of 47 Squadron, RAF Middle East, wrote the following letter.

Dear Mrs Muller-Rowland

I am writing to tell you the circumstances in which your son, Stanley, is missing.

We were carrying out essential but extremely hazardous operations against enemy shipping in the Aegean Sea, and Stanley who had only just left his Squadron after doing a magnificent tour of duty, came back to help us as our crews were hard pressed. He flew up to this Squadron one morning and volunteered for an operation in the afternoon. He led a formation of aircraft to attack JU 88s somewhere between Leros and Patnos. In the course of pressing home his attack, it seems clear he was hit in one or both engines by the rear guns of the JU 88s. He made a perfect controlled landing in the sea and got into the aircraft dinghy and in the end was seen floating a hundred yards or so from the shore. There can be therefore, little doubt that he reached the shore alive and well, although of course we expect that he fell into enemy hands.

I had known him personally for some four or five months and in fact had done several operations with him. He was in another Squadron, but on one occasion we did a joint effort. I led the contingent from my Squadron and he conducted the whole operation. He was a fine leader indeed. He had a great enthusiasm for operations as anybody I have ever known, and we all liked him immensely. Knowing his great spirit, I feel sure he will be turning up again one of these days.

His kit has been gathered together by his friends and forwarded to the Standing Committee of Adjustment who will communicate with you.

If there is anything further, I can tell you will you please let me know.

Yours sincerely

A Smith, Flight Lieutenant

It was reported in the Roll of Honour in the Daily Papers that Stanley was posted missing, and a week later it was reported that Stanley was safe.

On 27th November, Daisy received a telegram from the Air Ministry to say information had been received that Stanley had left Ankara on 22nd and that he had returned safely to the Middle East. This was not strictly true as on 29th Stanley sent his mother a telegram from Izmir, Turkey to say he was well and enjoying life.

On 5th December Stanley joined course No 12 at the Advanced Bombing and Gunnery School at RAF Ballah. Stanley's first flights were to familiarise him with the single engine aircraft which by this time were more powerful than those singles he had flown previously. On the 6th, flying in North American Harvard AT820 he carried out local flying with an instructor. From the Harvard he then gained experience in the Hawker Hurricane on the 7th and the Supermarine Spitfire on the 10th. The course consisted of mainly air to air firing at drogues being towed by a Harvard. On 13th December Stanley took part in a Bomber Co-Operation exercise carrying out quarter attacks. This involved coming in towards the target from slightly to one side and on an angle, to enable the gunners in the bombers to train their guns on a target. With Sergeant Lyne as passenger/ instructor Stanley had a demonstration flight in a Harvard to teach him the art of towing the drogue. Interspersed with a few bombers co-operation exercises air to air gunnery was to be much of the course in both the Hurricane and Spitfire apart from the last few flights when he was doing air to air firing with the Beaufighter.

On passing out from the course on 2nd January 1944 Stanley's assessment was Marksman Air-to-Air ----Exceptional. Marksman Air-to-Ground ----Average. Marksman Air Combat ----Average and Instructor

----Exceptional. A total of 18 hours flying was clocked up during this short period. Returning to 5 METS on 2nd January, Stanley continued flying as a torpedo, bombing and gunnery instructor carrying out numerous demonstrations for other aircrews to watch. His job took him to various bases throughout the region, so he did not spend all his time at Shallufa.

On 8th January, a bomber co-operation exercise took place, to enable the new crews to understand the way to operate when flying as an escort or to allow the gunners the opportunity to learn the skills of their trade. As an aid, cinefilm was used to record the events which was then played back to the student pilots once they returned to base. Mistakes could then be rectified on subsequent flights. A lesson that had been learnt the hard way by a few crews was that of landing with just one engine, this had not been covered that well at the OTU's. This was something that Stanley had experienced a few times so was in a good position to teach other pilots. In early February Stanley was teaching low flying over the sea and demonstrating as before. In the same way as the bomber co-operation exercise, cinefilm was used to record the Rocket Projectile (R/P) attacks, which again would be played back to the trainees.

On 15th Bob Willis, one of the pupil pilots flew with Stanley on a night torpedo training flight. They carried out a simulated torpedo attack on the 1st Battle Squadron, RN, who were conducting an exercise. Mock attacks were carried out in conjunction with a Wellington bomber who acted as a flare dropping aircraft. As the attacking aircraft approached so the target flares would be dropped to illuminate the ship and the pilot would then be able to line up on his torpedo run. All this time a camera was running to record the results. As the Beaufighter only had a crew of two there was only one seat up front for the pilot so any trainee pilot would have to stand behind the pilot to study his movements. The chief difference between these training flights and the real thing was the lack of anti-aircraft fire on training.

Being used to flying twin engine aircraft, an interesting change for Stanley, occurred on 23rd March 1944. As part of his role at 5 METS, Stanley took part in an anti-tank exercise, flying Hurricane MkIV KX406. The Hurricane was armed with 25lb R/Ps. As an instructor in the use of R/P's Stanley adapted his skills to fly single seat aircraft on the same of mission.

In June *HMS Victorious* and *HMS Indomitable* were provided by the Royal Navy as the targets for an exercise in which Stanley was flying in his, by now, normal place as formation leader. As part of the co-operation with the Navy some of the ship's officers would fly with the crews of the bombers to be able to appreciate what it looked like from the air and to better understand how to handle the situation should they come under attack by enemy aircraft.

Brian Quinlan, of 485 Squadron RAAF remembered being trained by Stanley while converting to the Bristol Beaufighter at Shallufa. His recollection was of Stanley being highly professional at work but always had a twinkle in his eye with a ready wit. Stanley's time at METS came to an end on 16th July when he received a posting back to the UK. During his time at 5 METS, Stanley had clocked up 52 hours on single engine aircraft, 90 hours daytime flying on multi-engine types and 25 hours night flying, making a total of 167 hours in the ten months he was there. He now had a grand total of 910 hours since he joined the RAF.

Stanley joined the North Coates Strike Wing on 30th August. A Wing consisted of three squadrons of Beaufighters. The first to attack was armed with cannon, to suppress the enemy anti-aircraft fire; the second armed with R/Ps would go into the attack before the torpedo armed Beaufighters launched their assault. Stanley was in the torpedo-armed 236 Squadron, tasked with the job of attacking German shipping coming down the North Sea coast bringing raw materials from Sweden and Norway. These convoys were carrying the desperately needed iron ore for the German factories. Leaving Norway, they would run the gauntlet between there and Rotterdam.

Most of the missions undertaken by the Beaufighters were at night as during the day the convoys would hide up in the fiords while they were in that area. Some of these fiords were narrow with steep sides making attacks extremely difficult. These convoys were heavily protected by flak ships and fighter cover due to the importance of getting the materials to the German-held Dutch ports. After an air test on 31st August and R/P firing practice on 1st and 2nd September, Stanley crewed up with Flight Lieutenant Alan Kendall who became his regular navigator. Stanley's first operation was an armed sweep from Lister to Eigeroy with sixty aircraft on the 3rd. Thirteen aircraft of 236 Squadron along with aircraft from 254, also of the North Coates Wing, rendezvoused with the Langham Strike Wing and their fighter escort over Strubby. The mission was to carry out a reconnaissance in force to the Norwegian coast. Although four ships were sighted Squadron Leader Wilson called off the attack as one vessel was a hospital ship. The next sweep was on the 6th when Stanley led forty aircraft, made up of fourteen aircraft of the North Coates wing and the Langham wing for an early morning patrol ranging from Borkum to Heligoland. Nothing was seen so all aircraft returned to base.

The difficulty with sweeps like this was the fact that the convoy may well have been alerted by the previous reconnaissance aircraft in which case they would seek the protection of the rugged coastline. Also, the weather would play a large part. Similar bad luck was to be had on the 9th when as deputy strike leader, Stanley and eleven other crews of 236 Squadron along with twelve crews from 254, picked up their fighter escort at Coltishall and set course for the Dutch coast. Although several vessels were seen – five at Terschelling and fifteen at Borkum – no attack was made due to bad weather and poor light.

An attack on shipping at Terschelling , on the 10th, by the combined forces of North Coates and Langham Wings resulted in five ships being attacked and damaged but no further results were seen due to the evasive action taken while getting away from the target area. The anti-aircraft fire was heavy. Exiting over land the force attacked land-based installations with Stanley silencing an anti-aircraft position on the southern tip of Terschelling and another destroyed by other crews. On the return journey Stanley circled the blazing wreck of Flight Sergeant Kimberley of 254 Squadron and his navigator. Flight Sergeant Macnee of 236 Squadron's aircraft, fixed and reported the position and gave air cover until a Vickers Warwick arrived to take over this duty. The aircraft remained until an Air Sea Rescue aircraft or launch arrived to pick up the survivors.

The squadrons of the strike wing noticed extraordinarily little let up in the number of raids they undertook. The pressure on the German supplies had to be kept up, if not the convoys would get through. Even the threat of Coastal Command's attacks kept the pressure on and slowed down the supply of raw materials.

Up again on the 12th, a convoy of nineteen vessels in Den Helder was the target. This convoy had by this time split down. With ten aircraft each from 236 and 254 along

81

with the Langham Wing, fighter escort Wing Commander E W "Bill" Tacon DSO, DFC, AFC, led the raid. A large MV was hit many times by RP's and cannon fire. The final tally was the loss of five vessels, two of which were seen to be burning fiercely. Again, on the return journey, flying out over island of Texel, Stanley took the opportunity to shoot up anti-aircraft positions, an RDF station, and a barracks. He also attacked the two-gun sites which were destroyed, the RDF station which was badly damaged and unusable without repairs being made and the barracks which were badly damaged. They met intense light and heavy anti-aircraft fire during the attack which brought down two of the formation and damaged the port main-plane, engine, and fuselage of Stanley's aircraft.

Wing Commander Tacon and his navigator Flying Officer G W H Wardle failed to return from this operation. Wing Commander Tacon was blown out of his aircraft when it exploded, although severely burnt he managed to pull the rip cord on his parachute and landed on Texel to become a prisoner of war. Flying Officer Wardle had been killed before the explosion.

On the 13th Stanley had led 236 Squadron on a sweep round Heligoland Bight where they found four ships at anchor and encountered heavy anti-aircraft fire from shore and ship installations. With extremely poor light and bad weather the raid was aborted.

On the 17th, Stanley led a strike on armed trawlers, southeast of Heligoland, they obtained cannon and R/P hits on one of the trawlers which blew up and sank. The other ship was very severely damaged. Again, heavy anti-aircraft fire was evident with Stanley's NT950 sustaining damage to the port main plane, but all the aircraft returned to base.

A fruitless sweep from Lister to Christiansand (Kristiansand) resulted in the sighting of a small Danish fishing fleet 50-100 miles from the Norwegian coast. As these posed no threat and were not the type of shipping to help the German war industries the Wing headed for home. The squadrons were diverted to Tain, Scotland due to bad weather.

The weather was a major factor in whether a raid could be successful or not. As the autumn draws on so the weather over the North Sea tends to close in. In some cases, aircraft could leave their bases with clear skies and good visibility only to find that the target was totally obscured by cloud. For this very reason, no flying took place on the 20th, 21st, or 22nd. The main attack of the 23rd was planned for the areas of the Zuider Zee and Den Helder. Forty aircraft from the various squadrons took part with an escort of Mustangs. At the time the leader called to bomb the shipping the fighters were not in place to provide the protection needed and so he called off the attack.

Taking advantage of the fact they were already over enemy territory they attacked a Radio Direction Finding (RDF) station on the coast blowing the top of the mast off with cannon fire. Several gun positions were targeted with two set on fire and others severely damaged. Finally, an anti-aircraft gun tower was shot up with RP's and cannon fire. At Wing strength, a strike was made on a convoy of twenty ships off the coast of Den Helder. Again, fighting through both light and heavy anti-aircraft, fire the Wing caused substantial damage, but at the cost of four Beaufighters. On the way back from enemy territory the Wing attacked a flak position and an RDF station.

The 25th was to be an extremely successful day for the forty-one aircraft from 236, 245 and the Langham Wing that took part. Twenty vessels were seen stationary in the harbour at Den Helder. It was agreed that part of the force would operate inland to attack various positions and to divide the attention of the anti-aircraft gunners on shore. Good results were seen by those that took part. As for the remainder, with RP's and cannon they caused extensive damage amongst the ships. The aircraft flown by Flight Sergeant Savage and his navigator was hit and badly damaged but with great skill and determination he made it back to base and landed safely with neither of the crew injured. The last two sweeps carried out by Stanley in September proved to be uneventful with only small vessels being sighted on the 28th and nothing at all seen on the 30th.

On 3rd October 1944 Stanley took part in his final strike, flying the Bristol Beaufort X NT950 MB-T taking off from RAF North Coates, Lincolnshire at 0018 on the night of 2nd October as one of six aircraft to locate and attack an enemy convoy of eight M/Vs off the coast of Holland. The aircraft were armed with 8x25lb rocket projectiles and 4x20mm cannons for this raid. Due to poor weather conditions only three of the six Beauforts managed to locate the convoy. Pilot Officer Hames in NE766 returned to base with engine failure soon after leaving the coast. Flying Officer Thompson in NT897 first sighted the convoy at 0156 but was unable to attack due to bad weather. He sighted the convoy again at 0236 and managed to attack this time with RPs and cannon.

In the meantime, Stanley had seen the convoy and attacked as had Flying Officer Middlemass in NV293. Intense and accurate anti-aircraft fire was encountered which meant that no results could be observed on any of these attacks due to the need to take evasive action. At 0300 Flight Sergeant Prince in NE799 and Lieutenant Nemerov in NT991 received a message from Stanley's navigator to say they were preparing to bale out. This was the last that was heard of them. Stanley's aircraft had been hit in the starboard engine. Although Prince and

Nemerov had not been able managed to locate the convoy they were still in the area. Flight Sergeant Wellstead, Prince's navigator passed this message to Chatham. On landing back at North Coates two of the crews reported the Anti-Aircraft fire was intense and accurate making the attack extremely difficult. The remaining aircraft landed back at North Coates between 0330 and 0410. NV293 had received battle damage to the port aileron but managed to land safely. A search was carried out, but no wreckage was found and no traces of their bodies.

(Authors note, from the details of the last reported position of Stanley and Alan's aircraft, Netherlands Hydrographic have charted the approximate location of the wreck about 11k northwest of Terschelling in 20-30 metres of water. It is in an area of shifting underwater sand dunes so may not be visible at all times, depending on the sand).

Enquiries to the Dutch authorities after the war led to nothing. The convoy attacked was No 1291 and the 1923-ton ship, Hanse-Neuban was sunk in the attack. The other aircraft involved were Flying Officer A Thompson and Flying Officer D J Savage in H NT897, Flying Officer R L Middlemas and Flight Sergeant J Dugdale in G NV293, Lt Nemerov (American) and Flying Officer H Lowe in A NT991, Flight Sergeant Prince and Flight Sergeant C F Wellstead in W NE799 and Pilot Officer R H B Hames and Pilot Officer A H Smith in O NE766.

The statistics show that the losses among the aircrews that undertook the type of low-level attacks used in the anti-shipping role suffered a five to one ratio of losses from anti-aircraft fire compared with those in higher level attacks.

On the same day that Stanley was shot down near Patmos two other aircraft had been lost. 603 Squadron

Beaufighter, LX977 developed an oil leak in the starboard engine, and when the engine cut out the pilot, Warrant Officer Cox, was forced to ditch in the sea. Landing on the water tail first the aircraft was soon swamped by the waves and the tail broke away. Warrant Officer Ferguson managed to leave the aircraft and was seen in the water about 50 yards from a dinghy, which he had no chance of reaching in the rough conditions. Stanley, with two other aircraft remained on station for half an hour, but nothing more was seen of Ferguson. Cox had failed to escape. 403722, RAAF, Warrant Officer Frank Mitchell Cox, aged 22, was the son of Frank Garnet Cox and Mabel Jane Cox of Darling Point, New South Wales. 400984, RAAF, Warrant Officer Norman Stewart Ferguson, aged 27, was the son of Dr Stewart William and Amey Esh Ferguson of Melbourne, Victoria. Both men are commemorated on Column 227 of the Alamein Memorial, Egypt.

A third aircraft lost on this sweep was LZ127 of 47 Squadron, at 0955 this aircraft was shot down north of Levitha, by Leutnant Emil Clade of 7/JG57 flying a Messerschmitt 109. The crew were, J/13088, Flying Officer Edgar Leroy Clary, RCAF, aged 23. Edgar was the son of Edgar L and Norma L Clary of Chippewa Falls Wisconsin. Edgar's navigator was, 1380965, F/Sgt Walter Edwin Fimbow, RAFVR, aged 22. Walter was the son of Walter Henry and Elsie Emily Finbow of Lee, London. Edgar is commemorated on Column 271 and Walter is on 269 of the Alamein Memorial.

In 1952, Daisy received a letter from the Imperial War Graves Commission. It appears that not long before being killed, Stanley had been recommended for the Air Force Cross. As he was posted missing before this could be actioned it could not be awarded as the criteria stated that it was not possible to make this award posthumously, hence it was revoked.

The full listing of aircraft types flown by Stanley is at Annexe A.

The Battle of Leros.

With the fall of Greece and Crete in April 1941 the British were deprived of the use of these bases to cover the Mediterranean. The Italians took control of the smaller islands and as with all the islands in the region, control of these was crucial to maintain Rommel's supply routes to North Africa. With its deep port, Leros provided a substantial naval base under Italian control. When the Italians surrendered on 8th September 1943 the British took control and strengthened the garrison on the island. This posed a threat to German shipping so it was vital that the Germans should try to gain Leros and the other Greek Islands.

The bombing campaign began on 25th September and continued until 11th November. Under constant pressure the defenders were running low on food and ammunition, with re-supply difficult because of the constant German air activity. The RAF made many sweeps around the island to keep the German forces at bay and, on the day that Stanley was shot down, they downed three JU52 transport aircraft carrying paratroops, but the defence proved unsuccessful. On 12th November the Germans managed to land paratroops on Leros and the British forces surrendered on 16th November.

CHAPTER 5

The Crews

Although the Muller-Rowland brothers are the main focus of this book we must not forget that their experiences and fates were shared with their crews, the men they flew with. Alan James Kendall was the navigator for Stanley Muller-Rowland and Ernest William Alexander was Eric Muller-Rowland's navigator.

151864, Flying Officer Alan James Kendall

Alan James Kendall, the son of Alfred Berry Kendall (1878-07/08/1930) and Emily Oliphant Kendall (Critchley) (1879-1960), was born on 9th May 1910 in Gorton, near Manchester, Lancashire. Alan had two brothers and two sisters, Eric Critchley, 1908-1984, Marjorie, 8/12/1911-12/10/1972, Denis Railton, 18/2/1915-1989 and Lenore, 23/5/1916-1998.

In 1927, Alan joined William Deacon's Bank where he worked in the Cheadle Branch, leaving in 1942 to join the RAF. On 14th October 1939 Alan married Margaret Edith Humphreys, (1911-2002), at Norbury, Chester. In the 1939 Register Alan (national registration number NJVD 229/2) is listed as a Bank Clerk. By this time Alan's father had died and the family lived at 20 Birch Grove.

Prior to Alan's enlistment in the Royal Air Force on 26th February 1942, Alan had been a member of the Air Training Corps. He took his medical that day and passed

Alan Kendall in Canada

as grade 1 medically fit for training as air crew. Alan became a navigator, a role that he became exceptional at. It was highly likely this was the reason he was crewed up with the highly professional Stanley Muller-Rowland. His record shows that he was 6ft 1 ½ in height, fair haired with grey eyes and a fresh complexion. He was posted to No 3 Receiving Centre at RAF Padgate near Warrington and placed on the Reserve. It was on 20th April when he went to the Air Crew Reception Centre. Passing through a couple of training establishments, he was eventually posted to 31 Personnel Despatch Centre prior to his departure to Canada where he arrived on 30th December 1942. Here Alan attended 33 Air Navigation School at Hamilton, Ontario, Canada. Alan carried out his navigational training on the school's Avro Ansons. On completion of his course, Alan moved to the School of General Reconnaissance on 17th July 1943.

Alan had applied for a temporary commission which was granted on 26th June 1943 when he was discharged from the Royal Air Force and transferred to the Royal Air Force Volunteer Reserve as a Pilot Officer. Alan's next move was to 132 Operational Training Unit (OTU) at RAF East Fortune, East Lothian, Scotland. The unit at this time was equipped with the Bristol Blenheim and Bristol Beaufighter as part of Coastal Command. It was while he was at East Fortune that he did a Signals Course. Alan was posted to 236 Squadron on completion of his time at OTU. Only a month after joining the squadron Alan was promoted to Flying Officer.

Alan's first operation on joining the squadron was on 8th October, in Beaufighter ZH-W LX982 with pilot Flight Lieutenant P D Mitchell when they carried out an unsuccessful patrol from North Coates. Another patrol on the 13th was equally unsuccessful when they returned due to bad weather. The weather over the North Sea was changeable which caused havoc with the flying of reconnaissance missions. Many days flying was lost in October due to the bad weather and Alan only took part in the two missions that month. Although it is difficult to be certain, he may have taken part in some other operations as the Operations Record Book (ORB) states that on some days aircraft from the squadron took part in wing raids no individual aircraft or crews are listed.

November 1943 was little better. On 5th November twelve aircraft, operating in pairs, took off for a series of patrols. Taking off at 1220hrs, Alan, with Flight Lieutenant Mitchell at the controls of ZH-Y LX845 was due to fly with Flight Sergeant Stacey and Sergeant Morris in LX856, to patrol over the North Sea. LX856 failed to take off due to engine failure leaving Flight Lieutenant Mitchell to continue the patrol alone. The other aircraft had already left the RV Point with the fighter cover. Sixteen Beaufighters of 254, and eleven from 236 Squadrons, took off on the 16th to carry out patrols in the region of Den Helder.

Ten to twelve ships were sighted in an orderly formation. On returning, aircraft were somewhat dispersed with two having already returned to base with engine failure.

Alan Kendall in uniform

One landed at Coltishall and Mitchell, with Alan, landed at Grimsby. The weather had closed in making visibility difficult. After two more missions that were aborted due to bad weather and poor visibility the squadron had greater success on 23rd when as a Wing strike with aircraft from 245, five Torbeaus (Torpedo armed Beaufighters) and ten other aircraft of 236 Squadrons attacked a convoy of about twelve enemy vessels to the north of the island of Texel.

The convoy consisted of ships of various sizes including a tanker of between 8 and 10,000 tons, with defensive cover on either side. Mitchell with Alan in V LX845 attacked two of the smaller vessels. One aircraft was lost and two others severely damaged with one making a forced landing at base with the under carriage failing to lower. The claims for this raid were:

- One tanker severely damaged by torpedoes.
- Two of the smaller vessels were seriously damaged and set on fire with two more partially damaged.

Although the squadron took part in many raids during December, I cannot find any record of Alan flying during the month. The squadron did manage to achieve more missions, with fewer days lost due to the weather. A substantial amount of damage was inflicted on German shipping off the coast of Holland during this time.

The next record of Alan flying is on 24th January 1944, when fifteen aircraft from 236 and twelve aircraft from 254 Squadrons, took off for a patrol in the areas of Juist to Borkum. Once out over the North Sea the aircraft encountered heavy rainstorms which limited the visibility. No shipping was sighted so the formation headed for home with all aircraft landing safely back at base. This is the only time in January that Alan and Mitchell were involved in any ops. Once more February proved to be a month in which Alan had limited flying. Of the one large raid he was due to go, Alan was unable to take off when his aircraft along with two others suffered engine failure.

On 7th March fifteen aircraft from 254, nine aircraft from 143, and six aircraft from 236 Squadrons left North Coates for a recce in force operation. All of the aircraft were armed with RP's and cannon. Airborne at 1429hrs in "M" K4280 Squadron Leader Mitchell, with Alan as his navigator, led the squadron's aircraft in formation with those from the other squadrons. At 1718hrs the formation sighted a convoy of 6-8 small ships. The aircraft turned in to attack the convoy with both RP's and cannon. Mitchell first attacked a coaster at the rear of the convoy and followed this with an attack on another vessel. Several cannon strikes were observed on both vessels, but the ORB does not state what damage was caused to them. The other aircraft followed suit and attacked various ships causing much damage with RP strikes and cannon fire.

"N" flown by Australian Flight Sergeant D P O'Donoghue with Pilot Officer DNG Sinclair as navigator did not attack due to flak damage, although no injuries had been sustained by the crew. One other aircraft received several hits from flak, again with no injuries to the crew. All aircraft landed safely back at base between 1825hrs and 1847hrs.

The visibility was poor over the North Sea on the 11th March when ten aircraft, supplemented by a further sixteen from the other two squadrons, left for another recce in force. The visibility closed in to 1000 yards and the leader, Mitchell, could only see his ten aircraft and six fighters. The Wing set course for base having aborted the raid. One more aborted raid took place on the 21st which was Alan's last flight for March.

Looking at squadron records Alan was obviously a highly competent navigator as he was very often with the squadron commander in the lead aircraft. No doubt with his experience Alan would have spent quite a lot of time teaching the finer details of navigation to new crew members coming into the squadron. Alan's role as navigator also entailed keeping look out to the rear of the aircraft for enemy fighters and manning the rear firing defensive guns. With no flying logbook to refer to, it is difficult to piece Alan's RAF service together accurately.

Towards the end of March or early April Mitchell had been promoted to Wing Commander and assumed command of the squadron. On 14th April, flying "Y" NE342 Mitchell led a recce in force to locate a convoy that had been sighted earlier. On route two minesweepers were spotted and the leader turned to investigate. It was decided to continue the patrol to locate the convoy. A fighter escort had been allocated for this raid as had some Torbeaus but these could not be seen. After an extensive search there was no sign of the convoy, so Mitchell abandoned the patrol and detached part of the flight to attack the minesweepers. By this time, the minesweepers could not be found either.

Airborne at 1522hrs on 18th April, Mitchell with Alan, led nine aircraft of 236 with another eight from 143 and seven from 254 Squadrons on a wing recce in force. At, 1710hrs two vessels were sighted, and the Wing attacked from between 800 and 1000 feet. Using RP's and cannon one of the ships completely disappeared and the other was left on fire and emitting a large cloud of smoke leading to a claim that it was probably destroyed. Anti-aircraft fire from the leading vessel was heavy but inaccurate and that from the other ship was lighter but also missed its targets.

On the 20th April another recce in force proved successful when ten aircraft took off at 1620hrs. One motor vessel was seen with three escorts. The attack left all the ships with damage and many hits were observed. The defensive anti-aircraft was light from the escorts but the coastal batteries at Schiermonnikog put up a heavy barrage. One aircraft failed to return. This was the last flight for Alan in April, although the Squadron did carry out more raids when weather permitted.

It must have been infuriating for crews risking their lives so often going out on the sweeps over the sea, which was a hazard in itself, but to spend a few hours flying and not see anything to attack must have made them wonder if it was worthwhile. Alan took part in five missions in May and only the first had any success when a convoy was attacked, and the ships damaged, but the cost was several aircraft damaged and their crew members wounded. The rest of the squadron had mixed results throughout the month.

In June Alan only took part in two sorties both of which were from Manston, Kent and both proved uneventful. The squadron itself took part in many more raids with mixed results. These patrols from Manston were a break away from the normal North Sea patrols the squadron had been conducting. This was to protect the eastern end of the English Channel to prevent the interference of the Allied landings in Normandy.

July 1944 was a busy month for the squadron looking at the record of events, with a heavy commitment undertaking anti-shipping patrols off the Norwegian and Dutch coasts. Of the sorties Alan flew in July the only one that was of any note was the first. On the 5th, flying with Wing Commander Mitchell, Alan was lead navigator for a force of thirteen aircraft from 236 and ten from 254 Squadrons armed with RPs and six more from 254 Squadron armed with torpedoes. At 0537hrs a convoy was spotted consisting of one large vessel and a few smaller ones. The formation attacked with RPs and torpedoes setting the larger ship on fire and severely damaging nine or ten of the smaller ones. Accurate anti-aircraft fire was encountered, and one aircraft failed to return and a second one suffered engine damage but managed to return to base. The raids on the 9th, 10th, and 16th were uneventful with only two Dutch fishing boats spotted on the 16th. Alan flew three more sorties after this one in which he flew as navigator to Wing Commander Tacon when they encountered heavy fire from shore batteries on the Dutch coast and on the 26th they attacked two smaller enemy vessels just off the Dutch coast.

August was to be somewhat nomadic for the squadron. Moving some of its aircraft for a detachment to Thorney Island, Sussex and then moving to Davidstow Moor, Cornwall. On 12th August, Wing Commander P D F Mitchell, flying NT953 with Alan as his navigator, took off with eleven other aircraft at 1052hrs from Davidstow Moor. Armed with 8x 25lb and 8x60lb RP's and 4x 20mm cannon along with twelve aircraft from 404 Squadron they set off for an anti-submarine patrol. On the journey out Mitchell, who was leading, spotted an enemy merchant vessel and one escort. It was decided to leave these and continue the patrol which turned out to be unsuccessful. On the return journey the merchant ship and its escort were seen again, and this time attacked. Many hits were sighted, and the vessel blew up aft of the bridge. The escort vessel put up an intense barrage of anti-aircraft fire and the Beaufighter S WT952, flown by Flight Sergeant R F Hollands with his navigator Flight Sergeant P B Osborne was shot down. The crew took to their dinghies and were rescued by the Royal Navy (RN).

The (RN) had been directed to the downed airmen by another pilot from 236 Squadron.The RN vessel then proceeded to the burning hulk of the Speerbrecher and sunk it with gunfire and torpedoes. Hollands and Osborne were landed back on the 14th. Following a move to St Eval in the afternoon of the 22nd in preparation for a sortie to the French coast near the river Gironde, eleven aircraft took off at 1906hrs with Mitchell and Alan leading. Two aircraft were forced to abort due to problems and the remainder set course for the target area. On nearing the patrol line, the weather had closed in and Mitchell was forced to abandon the operation.

As a result of the weather closing in over Cornwall the squadron became dispersed with three aircraft landing at St Eval, two at Predanack and one at St Mawgan. All aircraft returned to Davidstow the following day. The move to Cornwall was towards the end of Operation Cork, a measure to prevent the German Navy encroaching on the allied forces landing in Normandy. The squadron had been sending detachments to Davidstow since the early part of June. As a result of this operation the German Navy suffered heavy losses to its surface fleet and more so to its U Boat fleet.

Alan's last month of operations are covered in the chapter about Stanley.

On his service record it shows that after his death Alan was listed as being gazetted (entry in London Gazette) with the award of a Mention in Despatches on 1st February 1945.

Alan is commemorated on Panel 207 of The RAF Memorial, Runnymede.

A piece appears in the Manchester Evening News of 29th August 1945:

> "Alan James Kendall of 15 Mornington Road, Cheadle. Husband of Margaret, son of Mrs Kendall, of Birch Grove, Rusholme, previously reported missing now for official purposes presumed killed on active service".

Probate was passed on 11th January 1946 with his effects of £1139 6/ 6d passing to his widow. Margaret was a bank clerk in 1939 and joined the Red Cross. Post war she worked as the secretary to the Anglican Bishop of Jerusalem. Margaret died in Orkney on 25th January 2002.

958219, Flight Sergeant Ernest William Alexander.

Ernest William Alexander, one of two sons of Ernest Edward (1895-1976) and Annie Louise Alexander (Benson) (1901-1991) of Nottingham was born in 1921. Ernest also had a sister, Eunice F M born in 1923. He is commemorated on Panel 7 Column 1 of the Malta Memorial.

From the Nottingham Evening Post, 30th June 1943:

> "Flight Sergeant Ernest William Alexander of 60 Johnson Road is reported missing in North Africa".

On 9th November 1943 probate was passed with his effects of £143 6/ 7d going to his mother.

Unfortunately, I have not been able to trace any of Ernest's relatives to get more information about him.

Family comment on Alan Kendall

When David Parker first contacted me just over a year ago, he was wanting to know who my Uncle Alan's next-of-kin might be. This meant some research of my files on Ancestry to find out what had happened to his wife Margaret (nee Humphreys), who had inherited all of Alan's effects. She had died in 2002, and had never remarried nor had any children, and her six siblings were also deceased, so David and I decided to restrict our search to the Kendall side of the family. I was able to contact the two cousins of mine who are nieces of Alan and still living. In the end we decided that I, as the eldest, would be the one to sign the documents needed to allow publication of Alan's wartime history.

I was not yet two when Alan died, so not one of us three cousins can say we knew him. Nor do I recall my mother (Lenore), nor their mother (my grandmother Emily), ever talking about him, but my father knew him and liked him. It is from my father, with whom Alan shared an interest in machines, that I learned how Alan gave his little sister rides on his motorbike and helped her learn to drive a car. My father also taught me what a navigator like Uncle Alan did on an aeroplane, but he only showed me how to use my geometry set and maps – he didn't tell me about the frightening side of navigating while flying fast and low in wartime – it took a section in David's book to teach me this.

Now I look at the photograph taken at Alan and Margaret's wedding in 1939: it shows 57 people, of whom I recognise about 10, including my Uncle Denis, who was Alan's best man (just as Alan was best man when Denis and Mavis got married). Every single one of these people – and many more – would have mourned Alan's death in 1944. Like so many brave men who lost their lives in the war they were loved and would be missed, and they were *far too young to die.*

Leslie Barton, Toronto, February 2021

Alan and Margaret Kendall's wedding photograph

CHAPTER 6

Burma and India

While his brothers saw action nearer home much of Stuart's war service was spent far further east. After a brief period serving in North Africa, Stuart was sent to India with his Squadron. This chapter is not intended to be a definitive account of the Burma campaign, it is only to give an overview of that. For ease I have referred to British forces although this encompassed Indian troops. As will be seen later in the chapter about Stuart some of the places mentioned here also relate to his operations.

The defences of Burma had been left short for several years as it was thought unlikely that the Japanese would invade. Burma had been part of India until 1937, under British rule. Although the Governor of Burma was British the country had a fair amount of autonomy. Burma's position was vital to the Chinese who were still fighting the Japanese after they attacked China. Burma was the main route to keep China supplied. The United States of America (USA) had asked for pilots to volunteer to fight along-side the Chinese. The American Volunteer Group (AVG) needed Burma as this was the only way that its air bases in China could be maintained. This involvement of the USA was due to their supporting the Chinese during their on-going war against Japan. The second Sino-Japanese war began in 1937 and continued until the defeat of the Japanese forces in 1945. For India, the British remaining in Burma were the barrier the Japanese would have to cross to invade North-East India. If Burma fell, Calcutta and other industrial cities would be within the reach of Japanese bombers.

Burma was totally unprepared for war; with a small army and air force they would stand little chance against a determined attack. Although the Burmese army had seen some expansion the numbers were not great enough to repel an invasion. The British had only the 1st Battalion, the Gloucestershire Regiment and the 2nd Battalion of the Kings Own Yorkshire Light Infantry in Burma, and a number of men from both had been sent to India or back to the UK. All that could be mustered of these when the invasion came was barely more than two companies.

The air force situation was in an even worse state, with only 67 Squadron equipped with the Brewster Buffalo. With airfields at Victoria Point, Moulmein, Tavoy and Mergui. These were the vital links to Malaya, as the distances to be covered meant that aircraft flying to India needed to be refuelled at these airfields. Furthermore, these airfields were vital for bringing in reinforcements. In China, the AVG equipped with the Curtis Tomahawk, had been formed to assist in fighting the Japanese. Chiang Kai-Shek had given authority that some of these would be made available should Burma become threatened with invasion.

It was also in China's interest because this was a vital supply route for them too. Three squadrons had arrived by November and in December one squadron was assisting in the defence of Rangoon. Added to the air defence problem was the location of the airfields previously mentioned plus Rangoon, Toungoo, Heho and Namsung to Lashio in that they all were close to the border with Siam. There was no credible early warning system in place, just one RDF set and the Burmese Observer Corps which relied on the poor telephone network, which meant that the air forces started with a distinct disadvantage.

The Japanese had aircraft in greater numbers and with a far greater range than those of the British forces. Just before the Japanese invasion Chiang Kai-Shek offered General Wavell two Armies to help defend Burma. General Wavell accepted only one Division of the Chinese 6th Army, based on what became the flawed assumption that Malaya could be held. On 8th December 1941 Japanese forces invaded the Malay Peninsula in the north and pushed the British and Commonwealth forces down the peninsula to Singapore which fell on 15th February 1942, with the loss of many troops and equipment. Coinciding with this, the Japanese captured Bangkok on the same day, giving them total control of Thailand. This meant they had the all-important airfields from which they could launch air attacks against Burma. Railways and roads would enable them to move troops quickly in preparation to invade.

British and commonwealth forces were struggling at the time. The war in Europe had taken its toll with the loss of men and equipment at Dunkirk in May/June 1940 and the Battle of Britain in the summer of 1940. In North and North-East Africa, the war was being waged in the desert and the sea battles in the Atlantic were being fought by the Royal Navy against the German submarine menace as well surface ships. The upshot of these events culminated in the fact that there were simply not enough men or equipment to be sent to reinforce Burma. Allied to this was the great distance involved in getting the reinforcements to the region as they were unable to use the Suez Canal.

Rangoon came under air attack on 23rd December and a second attack followed on Christmas Day. The Buffaloes of 26 Squadron and Tomahawks of the AVG inflicted heavy losses on the Japanese with approximately 50 aircraft being shot down with the loss of 10 Buffaloes and 2 Tomahawks. The chief target had been the docks at Rangoon. When Burma came under attack many the Burmese people did not see what it had to do with them and wanted to avoid the war. Elements of the army and officials remained loyal to the British, but several politicians, rebels, students, and religious groups proved positively hostile.

As the invader progressed into Burma many members of the police, civilian services, and government officials deserted. The air raids caused many casualties and there were also a great number of refugees, mainly from some of the one million workforce from the docks at Rangoon. The Indians fled due to the actions of a faction of the Burmese army that had been trained by Japan prior to the outbreak of war. Once war was declared they came under Japanese control. Internally Burma was crumbling, with the Japanese taking advantage of the differences between some of the Burmese and the British.

On 15th January, within six weeks of the invasion to the north, a Japanese battalion crossed the border into Burma, taking Point Victoria on the 16th, Tavoy on the 19th and Mergui on the 23rd. This gave them the airfields in Burma from which their fighters could operate to escort the bombers to targets further into Burma. On the 28th Moulmein fell to the Japanese with the British forces, under Brigadiers Roger Ekin and Paddy Bourke, managing to escape by river steamer across the Bay of Martaban. 600 men were lost at Moulmein with a great deal of equipment. Shortly after this the 48th Gurkha Brigade, along with an armoured Brigade, were sent to Burma to reinforce those already there.

Withdrawal was the only option, with the defences in isolated positions the Japanese could infiltrate between these and out flank the defenders. Fierce fighting took place in the thick jungles, with two opposing armies only yards apart at times. On 19th February, the Allies started their withdrawal to the Sittang River by night. Breaking off engagements with the enemy so close was no easy feat. Thirty miles had to be covered to reach the river. On the 21st the troops had reached the Sittang Bridge, the only place to cross the river. Having been travelling for two days and nights the weary troops crossed the river before the demolition charges were set off on evening of the 22nd. There was a rear-guard who remained on the east of the bridge, many of whom swam across when the bridge was destroyed. Those troops not fortunate enough to have crossed the river were captured by the Japanese and became prisoners of war. The Sittang was a wide barrier between the two enemies which gave the allies some time. Once across the river the major task of feeding the troops, reorganising, and re-equipping them began.

Rangoon was now perilously close to being lost to the invaders and so the army commander, General Hutton, began his preparations for the inevitable. His engineers set charges to demolish the docks and oil storage facilities, evacuating the civilian population and all non-essential staff. As with many military operations an element of luck enabled the army in Rangoon to escape. The Japanese had allowed no flexibility in their planning and the commanders stuck rigidly to their orders. On 7th March, General Hutton gave the order to blow the charges, and the city was left burning as the last of the British troops boarded three ships that had been waiting for them after the final act of destruction of blowing up the port. When the Japanese entered Rangoon on the 8th, expecting a fierce battle, they found that the British had fled.

As the Rangoon affair unfolded plans were being carried out to evacuate the RAF. The RAF had been strengthened in February with units being brought in from India and North Africa to form "Burwing" based at Magwe, on the Irrawaddy. The wing consisted of 17 (fighter) Squadron, 45 (bomber) Squadron with its Bristol Blenheims (Stuart was flying with 45), along with 28 (Army co-operation) Squadron and a squadron of the AVG. Another smaller wing was based at Akyab, on the Bay of Bengal. By the 30th the withdrawal of the RAF was complete.

Now the army was retreating without air support. Suffering from Japanese air attacks the troops fought many hard battles and rear-guard actions, with a lot of dust and little water, into April, one of the hottest months in Burma. The capture of Toungoo at the end of March gave the Japanese a chance to plan their next big move, capturing Mandalay. The Chinese 65th Army were to the South of Mandalay where heavy fighting was taking place. It was obvious with the strength of the Japanese army and their air support that a prolonged stand to protect Mandalay was not going to be viable. On 26th April, the order was given for the army to fall back to protect India.

The commanders in the field began the retreat the same day. At Shwebo the American General J W Stilwell (known as 'Vinegar Joe'), with an element of the Chinese army, retreated on foot to the Chindwin River and on through the hills to Imphal, arriving in Assam on 15th May. Towards the end of the retreat, the rainy season started, causing several problems for the Allies but also a respite because the Japanese became bogged down. By mid-May the withdrawal was over. Although defeated in Burma and incurring great losses the troops had crossed into India. They were desperately exhausted and hungry, but they were still disciplined. Many were suffering from malaria and dysentery. Diseases in the jungles of Burma were to prove a major problem throughout the campaign for the next two years.

Thus, ended the longest retreat in British military history with nearly 1000 miles being covered. The losses were high: the British had lost with 3670 killed and wounded, and 6366 missing, many of which were taken prisoner of war and many of whom were to suffer the degradations of the Japanese POW camps. The Burmese lost 3400 bringing the allied total to 13463. The allies lost 116 aircraft. The Japanese casualties amounted to approximately 4597 killed and wounded and a loss of roughly the same number of aircraft as the allies.

With Rangoon and Moulmein in their possession the Japanese had control of the ports through which to move supplies. Furthermore, the railway from Rangoon to Myitkyina via Toungoo and Mandalay gave them the greatest asset.

The first venture back into Burma began on 21st September When Major General Lloyd led his 14th Indian Division from Chittagong via Cox's Bazaar to the Mayu Peninsular. The objective was to work his way down the peninsular to recapture the airfield at Akyab. The plan initially had been to land a force at Akyab to move north to join up with those progressing south. As it happened this plan was dropped, partly due to a shortage of vessels being available.

Transport problems had delayed Lloyd with heavy rain washing away what crude roads there were. Just one day in November thirteen inches of rain fell. By 1st December Lloyd's troops had taken a position on a line between Maundau and Buthidaung, on either side of the Mayu range of hills. The Japanese had pulled back from the line before the British arrived. The result was that the British had a free range of almost the entire peninsula. Lloyd's force followed up reaching Donbaik where the Japanese had dug in. This was a narrow point, so the Japanese forces were concentrated.

When the British arrived, they came under heavy fire from the concealed positions to their front in the dense bamboo. If this was not bad enough, they were also attacked from behind by Japanese troops who had been hiding in highly camouflaged, heavily concealed foxholes that had been over-run. The engagement at Donbaik was to last for three months, when in March the order came to retire to the coast. The British had got within a few miles of their first objective at Foul Point.

Meanwhile the British forces retreated to the Mayu range to take up new positions before the monsoon season started. These positions would be more sustainable and were held for the remainder of the year. It must also be remembered that the RAF played a significant role in support of this operation, so much so that the damage done to the sea and rail traffic significantly depleted the Japanese supplies. The Japanese soldiers were able to live off the land and so had this advantage but apart from that the Japanese army was in a more perilous state than the British.

The next venture into Burma was one of the most audacious actions carried out during the Second World War. Colonel Orde Wingate was a solitary man who had what some saw as rather strange ideas, because they were not textbook military tactics. Even as the first retreat was taking place Wingate had been developing a plan to take troops, trained in jungle warfare and demolition, behind enemy lines.

The military chiefs were sceptical about the whole idea, but Wingate had some reliable backing in the men he chose to lead the operation with him. His basic plan was to cause as much destruction as possible. The venture began on 8th February 1943 when Wingate's "Chindits" (a corruption of 'chinthe', Burmese for lion) split into two groups and entered Burma.

Crossing the Chindwin River and blowing up railway bridges from Mandalay to Mytkyina as they went, they worked their way towards the Irrawaddy before crossing this to form up in a triangle between a bend in the Irrawaddy and the Schweli. The whole operation relied on the RAF dropping supplies. The "Chindits" remained in Burma until 27th March when Wingate gave the order to retreat to India. The military success of this operation was limited but it had caused confusion within the Japanese high command who had not been suspecting an attack.

When the Japanese did realise something was happening, they sent troops to find and cut the supply lines but could not find any. It was only when a Japanese unit spotted an air drop that they realised how the British were being supplied. Two things that did emerge from this venture: firstly, proof that operations of this nature were possible, and secondly, they provided a valuable morale boost for the whole of the Allied forces.

Though seen as a success, of the 3000 officers and men who went into Burma, only 2182 returned. A ragged army with long beards, clothing in tatters, hungry and many suffering from malaria entered India, some still arriving in dribs and drabs two weeks later.

The second offensive into the Arakan began on 4th January 1944 when the British pushed forward from the positions, they had held through the monsoon season. This very nearly never happened as the Japanese had planned an attack and made the first move, which was held off by the British troops. The terrain in the Mayu Hills was dense bamboo jungle and streams that in dryer times only trickled down the hills but when it rained these became raging torrents which would prove unpassable. After fighting many fierce battles, the British recaptured Buthiduang on 11th March, regaining the line they had left the previous year.

Maundaw had been taken on 9th January so taking Buthiduang had given the British access to the road between the two places. In the meantime, the Japanese had launched Operation Ha-Go, which was intended to outflank the British and cut their supply lines from India. After many offensives and counter offensives this ended in defeat for the Japanese. This operation like that of General Wingate's "Chindit" operation was somewhat experimental and paved the way for future tactics. With the distances involved and the rugged terrain between India and Burma it was not possible to replenish supplies by road, so the force relied on air supply. The Royal Air Force, along with a small element of the United States Army Air Force dropped food and equipment in by parachute. These drops were not always successful as some fell into enemy hands due to being dropped in the wrong place or, with the situation on the ground changing rapidly, the drop zones had been overrun by the Japanese. During this campaign, the balance of airpower shifted. The Japanese had withdrawn aircraft for use in other theatres of operations, and the allies managed to gain air superiority.

By January 1944, the Allies had built up the air power to such an extent that the Japanese air force posed little threat in Burma. The British had 33 transport aircraft, 453 fighters and 64 bombers. The Americans had also expanded their air fleet to 51 transports, 141 fighters and 85 bombers. These were pitched against the Japanese who had no transport aircraft and had only 159 fighters and 96 bombers. The lack of air transport was because the Japanese had relied on waterways, road and rail transport to supply their troops. Bullock carts were often employed on the narrower tracks. As will be seen in the next chapter the supply lines of the Japanese were constantly being targeted.

With any campaign in Burma the problem was always that of supplying the troops. The rail system in India was geared up towards the north-west of the country. The north-east had no railway. Roads in this area were narrow and very few and of these none were good enough to stand up to the traffic that was required to supply an army. In Burma there were no roads at all. The only means of getting into Burma were via the few tracks through the dense jungle and mountain passes. For this reason, it had always been thought that the Chin Hills (rising to 12,000ft in some places), would provide a barrier between Burma and India. No attack was expected in this area and even the Japanese thought the hills and jungle to be unpassable. Air supply was to prove to be the vital lifeline for moving troops in, evacuating the wounded and supplying the troops in the next phase.

General Slim, commander of the British XIVth Army had been improving communications, building roads and supply dumps around Imphal. The Imphal plain is situated in the Manipur state, on the border of Assam. An extremely fertile area of around 700 square miles at 2500ft above sea level, the Imphal plain provided a vast amount of rice for the rest of India. The plain was bordered by the jungle-covered Chin and Naga hills, and was only seventy miles from the Burmese border, which was accessible by just one track through the mountainous jungle-covered terrain.

General Slim's improvements on the plain had not gone unnoticed by Japanese reconnaissance aircraft, so the Japanese rightly expected a British attack. As a direct result of Wingate's "Chindit" operation the Japanese expected that the British would plan a far larger attack than the one that had been anticipated earlier. The Japanese commander the XV Army in Burma, as early as October 1943 began planning his own attack with the intention of capturing Imphal and Kohima, to the north, which stood on a ridge 4,700ft above sea level. Crossing the Chindwin River at Homalin and Tamanthi with one place between, General Sato's XXXI Division headed for Kohima. General Yamauchi's XV Division moved to take Imphal from the north with General Yanagida's XXXIII Division coming up from the south to Imphal. This attack coincided with the planned British Arakan campaign.

Rapid advances followed with fierce battles being fought and the British forces retreating to Imphal which was besieged by the end of March/beginning of April. General Slim had put in place plans to resupply his forces by air. Initially there were not enough transport aircraft to cope with the demand but Admiral Louis Mountbatten, Supreme Commander, had persuaded higher authorities to provide more. The Japanese operation relied on the capture of Imphal and its supply dumps with their supply lines being extended and with only the narrow tracks over the Chin Hills. There was no provision for air supply. Bitter fighting took place over the next three months with heavy losses on both sides.

The British troops were short of food and ammunition while the Japanese suffered greater problems. The Japanese soldier had been used to living off the land, but sources of food was running short. The siege of Imphal continued until 18th July when the Japanese high command realised that the pursuit of any further attack would be in vain. The order to retreat was given. This did not bring to an end their troubles.

The retreat was long and arduous, with the British keeping up the pressure. By the time the retreat began the monsoons had started; the rivers were in full flood and the tracks became mud. Along the way the retreating forces found the tracks littered with the bodies of the wounded who had been sent back earlier but had not made it. Many more were to suffer the same fate. No provision had been made for supply dumps of food or medical supplies and with conditions as they were there was no possibility of help arriving. It was reported that in some cases, the Japanese were in such desperation they turned to cannibalism. The Japanese soldiers that crossed the Chindwin were mere skeletons dressed in rags, many with no footwear and no equipment. The effects of malnutrition and fatigue coupled with malaria, dysentery and beri-beri, caused by a lack of vitamin B1, all played their part. The men were not physically fit enough to carry anything. The soldiers had discarded their kit, many were barely able to walk even with the aid of a stick. This and the Kohima action were to mark the turning point in the Burma campaign.

At Kohima, the battle was fought in extremely close quarters. The British had retreated and consolidated by 5th April. There were many points of high ground that were heavily contested over the coming months. Steep terrain provided ideal vantage points for the Japanese who were heavily defended with numerous camouflaged bunkers.

With their supply lines cut the British at Kohima were in a more perilous situation than those at Imphal. Again, air drops were the only means of supply. The perimeter was only 1000 yards which meant that some of these drops accidently provided a small amount of relief to the Japanese troops when they landed outside this small area.

With the original plan for the capture of Imphal, General Sato was relying on the supplies to be sent by XV Division, but as Imphal had not been taken Sato's men had nothing. Repeatedly he contacted General Mutaguchi to request stores, but none were forthcoming. Sato's men fought on against relentless attacks and by 13th May defeat looked inevitable. The only strong points left were those at the Deputy Commissioner's bungalow and the tennis court with the bunkers dug into the high ground surrounding it. This was the bloodiest battle fought during the Second World War.

With defeat just round the corner and his men starving and desperately low on ammunition Sato took the decision to retreat without informing General Mutaguchi. For this one act Sato was blamed for the failure of the entire operation. In part the failure of the whole operation was down to the fact that some of Mutaguchi's officers had lost confidence in the plan. There was a lack of support in the way of fresh supplies and Mutaguchi refused to listen to his officers. For this reason, the entire operation was doomed to failure from the outset. Many of the officers could easily see the plan overstretched the limits of sustainability.

At the same time Mutaguchi was driven by loyalty, personal ambition, and honour. Many men from any army may well have had the same attitude and pressed on so as not to lose face once they were so heavily committed.

For the British, Kohima was one of those battles that would linger in many minds for many years, those who fought there being regarded as the bravest of the brave.

On the memorial at Kohima is the epitaph.

When You Go Home, Tell Them of Us and Say, For Your Tomorrow We Gave Our Today

Following Kohima General Wingate planned a second and much more ambitious "Chindit" operation, this involved 9000 troops. The first group had to march into the area of operations to prepare an airstrip. The whole operation was based on the remainder being taken into Burma by glider. General Slim had dictated the area where this should be conducted and laid down a set of tasks for the "Chindits" to carry out. These were to disrupt Japanese movements and cut supply lines and to divert as many Japanese troops as possible.

U S General Stilwell, with the Chinese, would assist by attacking from the north to divert the enemy. This had influenced the Japanese Imphal and Kohima attacks in that it diverted troops and resources from that area. On 5th March 1944, sixty-one gliders, towed by Douglas Dakotas took off for Burma. Disaster struck on the way and only thirty-five arrived – about a 45% loss of aircraft, men, and equipment that would leave the defenders much depleted. The weather took a massive toll on aircraft serviceability, and the harsh conditions also contributed to this. Many of those gliders that did not make it crashed on route. On hearing about the loss of the gliders General Mutaguchi did not take it seriously and took no action, not seeing this as a serious threat. This again points to the failure due to Mutaguchi sticking rigidly to his plan. One of the officers that had a totally different view was Lieutenant -General Tazoe. This also lays bare a previous piece where officers and men had lost confidence in their leader's ability to execute the operation to its ultimate conclusion.

The RAF had intensified their efforts beforehand and attacked his airfields destroying and damaging many aircraft on the ground. By 13th March 9000 men were in Burma. One of the brigades soon occupied an area of about 30 miles across straddling the only railway line to cause a disruption.

On 24th March General Wingate visited his commanders in the field. Taking off afterwards in a Mitchell B25 bound for India the aircraft crashed down into the slopes of the Bishenpur Hills killing all on board. Wingate, the man of vision had gone. The Chindits had carried out numerous attacks during their time in Burma supporting British actions which were to change on 9th April when the area of operations moved north to support Stilwell's push into Burma. The last "Chindits" left Burma for India on 27th August 1944.

The Japanese acknowledge the damage done by the "Chindits" more than the British. One commander spent a serious amount of time and effort chasing an enemy that was inflicting casualties on his troops but could not be found. Had this not happened the Imphal and Kohima campaigns would almost definitely have ended in defeat for the British, as it was, they were each a close-run thing.

With the RAF and General Slim's XIV Army maintaining constant pressure, the Japanese were driven back to the Chindwin and towards the Irrawaddy. Building up his forces at many points west of the Irrawaddy, Slim succeeded in deceiving the Japanese as to where the main force would be positioned.

By the beginning of February 1945, the British army started to cross the Irrawaddy, which was no easy task as the river was two miles wide in places. Once bridgeheads had been established the stage was set for the drive towards Mandalay. By the beginning of April, Mandalay had fallen after many bitter fights between the opposing forces.

The RAF needed airfields to be able to keep up with the army. New airstrips needed to be cleared from the jungle and existing airfields had to be captured. Roads and railways had to be constructed. Many engineer units were needed to carry out his work. If this could not be achieved the Japanese would have time to regroup. With the capture of Mandalay, Rangoon was the next major objective. In conjunction with an amphibious assault on 2nd May Rangoon was taken with little resistance on the 3rd. The end was in sight.

Many suicidal attacks and defences by the Japanese could not stop the advance. Continuing to retreat through June a very ragged Japanese army made a stand, with General Honda attempting a breakout on 19th July. This, instead of being a glorious attack, turned out to be a final desperate suicidal bid with only 96 allies lost against 11,500 of the 16,000 Japanese that took part. The last of the battles for Burma was over on 4th August.

CHAPTER 7

Stuart Muller-Rowland

As with Eric and Stanley, Stuart followed the same path in education: initially at Sunnydown, Hogs Back, Guildford from 1933-1935 and then to Uppingham School, Rutland from 1935 where he stayed on a year longer the Stanley, leaving in 1939.

Stuart was obviously studious, in July 1937 he attained credits in Scripture Knowledge, English, History, French (both written and oral), Physics and Chemistry. Stuart also studied German and Geography. Stuart was slightly more reserved than the out-going Stanley, although he did play rugby for his house at school. From 1936-1939 he was a member of the O.T.C. achieving the rank of Lance Corporal. With his ability and his School Certificate from The Oxford and Cambridge Schools Examination Board, Stuart did not have to sit the Preliminary Examination for the Institute of Chartered Accountants.

Stuart was "Highly Commended" for an essay he entered in the Gordon Shepherd Memorial Prize Essay Competition for 1948/1949. This was set up by Sir Horatio Shepherd in memory of his son Brigadier General Gordon Strachey Shepherd, DSO, MC. who was born in 1889 and killed in action on 19th January 1918. Shepherd was a commander in the Royal Flying Corps and the highest-ranking officer of the air services to be killed during the First World War. The prize is awarded annually to the serviceman/woman who writes the best essay on an air power topic.

Stuart on a motorbike

On 13th May 1939 Stuart boarded the *SS Markhor* of the Brocklebanks Wells Line, a ship of 7917 tons under command of the ships master, G C Douglas. Departing Portsmouth for Calcutta via Port Said, Suez, Aden, Tuticorin, Trincomalee and Madras, the ship arrived in Calcutta 100 days later.

1183350 John Stuart Rowland Muller-Rowland joined the Royal Air Force at R.A.F. Cardington, Bedfordshire with his brother Stanley on 29th July 1940. Stuart's civilian occupation was given as an Articled Accountancy Clerk with his National Insurance Number LT.537150B and his religion as Church of England.

The twins reported to No 9 Recruits Centre, Blackpool on 16th August and then to St Athan, Glamorganshire, Wales on 26th August. From late September Stuart undertook his initial training with No 3 I.T.W. passing out as Pilot under Training on 14th December. Stuart's initial flying training was with Stanley at 27 Elementary Flying Training School (E.F.T.S), Induna, Bulawayo where he flew the DH82 Tiger Moth. When he passed out from 27 E.F.T.S., he had completed 56 hours and 40 minutes flying and was classed as average.

Stuart was recommended for training on multi engine aircraft, so this meant his next posting was to 21 Service

Flying Training School (S.F.T.S), Kumalo, Bulawayo. After a further 50 hours on the Airspeed Oxford twin engine training aircraft, with above average grading, he was awarded his "wings" on 20th May 1941. During this initial flying training Stuart was promoted to Sergeant on 14th December 1940. He was discharged from the R.A.F. on 8th July 1941 and joined the General Duties Branch, Royal Air Force Volunteer reserve on a temporary commission for the duration of hostilities on 9th July as a Pilot Officer on probation with a new service number of 103497.

Stuart and Stanley's paths now parted with Stuart being posted to No 70 Operational Training Unit (O.T.U), Ismailia, Egypt on 15th July. From Stuart's logbook I can find no record of him flying between this date and the flight he undertook on 10th September in Bristol Blenheim Mk I -6631 on a familiarisation flight with Squadron Leader Burnett at the controls. His training here was on a mix of Blenheim Mk I's and Mk IV's. This consisted of formation flying at high and low level, high- and low-level bombing, dive bombing and air to air and air to ground gunnery practice.

Tests by the Chief Flying instructor took up much of his time here, with Stuart and his crew undergoing various exercises. It was here

Stuart in uniform

that Stuart crewed up with Pilot Officer Graebner and Sergeant Gardiner who were to stay with him in his next posting. Near disaster struck on 30th September when the port engine of Blenheim Mk IV V5880 failed, and Stuart was forced to make a wheels up landing 10 miles south of Nakuru. None of the crew were injured and they all flew together the following day.

(Authors note. The Bristol Blenheim was well known at the time for not being able to cope with the harsh desert conditions. This was also hampered by a lack of spares and facilities for the ground crews to service or repair their charges).

Classed as Average in navigation, bombing, and as a pilot with by now 219 hours of flying under his belt, Stuart was posted, along with his crew to the Middle East Pool prior their posting to No 45 Squadron on 16th October 1941.

The first flights on the Squadron consisted of local training and familiarisation flights. Stuart's first operational flight was on 22nd October when he left for a raid on the landing ground at Casa El Eyrid. Flying with his regular crew in Blenheim T2185, he was number 2 in the formation of six aircraft. On the 27th they left base at Fukas for the advanced landing ground of Landing Ground (LG) 53 in preparation for a raid on enemy supply dumps on the Tobruk-Bardia road. This was a flight of 3 hours 50 minutes.

On 1st November Stuart took part in a search for a downed aircrew. On the 2nd Stuart and his crew made a return visit in a night raid on the dumps along the Tobruk-Bardia road. As one of five aircraft Stuart took off from LG 53 at 1745 carrying a mixed load of bombs. The target had been lit up by Fairey Albacores of the Fleet Air Arm (FAA) with flares and incendiaries. Flying at 5000 feet bombs fell across the target and caused many explosions that could be seen for at least twenty miles. Any targets of opportunity that presented themselves got the full treatment of the attackers. As they were in the area, rather than return to base with ammunition left they would use it. A wooden hut was set on fire which was also machine gunned. Any of these seemingly minor things would deprive the Japanese of dry storage or accommodation, which was all important in the weather conditions that prevailed in Burma. All the aircraft returned safely, landing at 2145hrs.

The target on the 7th was Bir Hashim and its 350 motor vehicles and 60 tanks of Rommel's Afrika Corps. Another night attack, Stuart took off at 0230 with a load of 4x250lb bombs. Sticks of bombs were seen to fall right across the target with explosions seen and debris thrown up into the sky. One stick of bombs was seen to land close to the nearby landing ground. Once again, the target had been marked by the FAA Albacores. After a flight of 4 hours 15 minutes all aircraft landed safely back at base at 0704hrs.

Stuart did not take part in any more raids until 22nd November when he was flying one of six aircraft to attack Motor Transport (M/T) and tanks on the El Adem-Acroma road. The estimated time of arrival over the target was 1335hrs but they had to divert due to squalls of rain, so they did not arrive until 1405hrs. On this raid the aircraft were attacked by twenty Me 109s of JG27, with the Squadron losing four aircraft. The aircraft lost on this raid were Blenheim Mk IV's Z6439 crewed by Wing Commander J Willis DFC, Officer Commanding (O.C) 45 Squadron, Pilot Officer L Burke from New Zealand, and Sergeant M Carthy, all missing in action. Further deaths occurred among the other crews. Z7686 with Sergeant C O'Neil, Sergeant L Smith and Sergeant K Chapman were all lost. The crew of T2318, Sergeant C Melly, Pilot Officer L Rippingdale and Sergeant J Halsall were all captured and became prisoners of war. The last aircrew of Z9609 fared a little better although pilot Sergeant R Wood, and gunner Sergeant S Whiteley were taken prisoner. The navigator, Sergeant R Tutron, managed to evade capture and returned to the squadron. All these aircraft crashed in the vicinity of El Adem.

On the 24th with a fighter escort the four aircraft of 45 Squadron along with others from 14 and the Free French Lorraine Squadron set out to attack more M/T, this time on the El Adem-El Duda road. Once close to the target the aircraft attacked but all the bombs undershot with no damage being done. Heavy anti-aircraft fire was encountered but all aircraft returned safely. Again, on the 26th the target was M/T to the Northwest of Sidi Omar but due to 10/10ths cloud obscuring the target all aircraft returned with their bombs. On the 28th Stuart took part in another raid but did not write down the target in his logbook.

Although he had only been in the Squadron since the beginning of October 1941, he had clocked up a total of 24 hours and 25 minutes of operational flying. Many of the operations in the Middle East took place from advanced landing grounds so it was necessary to return to the base airfield to rearm, refuel and service the aircraft. For the remainder of November and December motor transport was the major target for many of the raids interspersed with attacks on supply dumps, often with a fighter escort.

On 4th December things did not get off to a good start when nine aircraft of 45 Squadron were due to take off with other aircraft from 14, 84 and Lorraine Squadrons to bomb M/T at Sidi Resegh. While taking off the aircraft of Sergeant Tolman collided with one from Lorraine Squadron. 5991 blew up killing Sergeant Tolman and his crew of Pilot Officer Hutton and Sergeant Harris. The

collision prevented four other aircraft from taking off.
Stuart had managed to get airborne before this incident.
The four remaining aircraft reached the target and made
a showing with three large fires started. The clouds of
black smoke could be seen over 45 miles away.

As part of a raid of six aircraft on the 12th, Stuart flew
from base to El Adem for a pre-flight briefing with the
fighter escort. The target was M/T on the Derna road.
Heavy anti-aircraft fire was encountered over the target,
but no real damage was sustained by any of the aircraft.
All returned to El Adem where they spent the night.

On 22nd December when Stuart was preparing to take
part in a raid after flying from LG 75 to Gambut and then
on to Gazala when he had to turn back due to engine
failure. The anti-aircraft defences were mixed with light
and heavy Anti-Aircraft (A/A) fire, some of which was
intense and accurate. For the remainder of the month,
the 27th, 28th 30th and two raids on the 31st the target was
M/T and pill boxes at Bardia. All these raids proved
successful with fires started and considerable damage
done. The only exception to this was on the 29th when six
aircraft took off to bomb Agedabia. The weather was so
bad at the rendezvous with the fighter escort it was
pointless to continue to the main target, so the decision
was made to return to Bardia with all the bombs
dropping amongst the M/T. Following a raid on dumps
at Bardia on 1st January 1942 Stuart went on leave on the
3rd. It was announced while Stuart was on leave that he
had been awarded the DFC.

45 Squadron was to change its role during the latter part
of January when on the 22nd Stuart, with Squadron
Leader Austin, flew to LG222 K17 along the Cairo-Fayoum
Road to collect the new heavily armed fighter/bomber
variant of the Blenheim Mk IV. These aircraft were
armed with cannon for ground strafing missions.

Practice in this new role was to take up most of the time until 13th February when the Squadron was to move to Burma. Taking their aircraft with them, the move was done in several stages with a total flying time of 23 hours 30 minutes arriving on 28th February.

Bomber operations in Burma had become effective from 7th January 1942, when 113 Squadron arrived from the Middle East with twelve aircraft. 60 Squadron had been posted to Malaya with the impeding threat of Japanese forces in the region. 60 had left behind some of their aircraft which were taken on strength by 113. With the arrival of 45 Squadron on 28th February they operated alongside 112 for a number of missions.

Commencing operations on 1st March, the squadron sent aircraft on a raid to a town near Waw. Flying in formation they attacked from 2000ft, no opposition was encountered. On the 2nd Stuart carried out an individual raid on the village of Sitang, again with no enemy opposition. This situation was to change, when on the 3rd a raid on M/T near Kayto was interrupted by the appearance of four Japanese Army fighters. The Blenheims dropped down low and got away with no losses. By 10th March after a concentrated series of operations in the preceding few days the Blenheim force was down to nine serviceable aircraft. 113 Squadron left Burma for Ceylon to re-equip leaving behind what aircraft it had.

Japanese troops and motor transport (M/T) and armoured fighting vehicles (AFV's) were the main targets for the next couple of weeks until 21st March when nine aircraft attacked the airfield at Mingaladon. The airfield was defended by fighters of the Japanese Navy and Army, which proceeded to attack the formation of Blenheims. During the ensuing fight two enemy aircraft were shot down with another two damaged. Stuart was wounded but got back to base with his damaged aircraft. On 29th

March, the entire Squadron was awarded a Mention in Dispatches for the Mingaladon raid on the 21st. The Squadron operations book states on the 26th that Pilot Officer Muller-Rowland was in Yenangyaung hospital following being wounded on 21st. Stuart's record is a bit vague as to what exactly happened and when, but it states he was admitted to hospital in Calcutta on 23rd April 1942, was discharged on 27th April, and then moved to the general hospital until he was discharged on 23rd May.

While Stuart was away from the Squadron the situation with the Japanese advance was such that the British bases were being over-run and the Blenheim force was much depleted with many of the squadrons being reduced to just a few aircraft. During Stuart's absence he was promoted to Flying Officer. Although there is no mention of it in Stuart's service record, he was attached to 60 Squadron on his return to operations. The official date for this was the 25th July 1942.

His first flight was on 29th July flying from Chittagong to Asansol to position his aircraft in preparation for ops. On the 31st he was flying Blenheim Z9828 with his crew of Pilot Officer Graebner and Sergeant Gardiner along with two other aircraft relocating to the forward base at Cuttack because it was suspected that a Japanese cruiser was operating in the Bay of Bengal. The detachment returned to Asansol on 11th August. Stuart's first operation was on 13th August when he carried out a reconnaissance and message dropping mission to the Patina area, flying at 50ft. In this region of Bengal there was the possibility of civil unrest amongst the local population due to anti-British feeling.

The Japanese policy had been to take advantage of the resentment to the British Empire felt by a number of Indians with the aim of encouraging the local population

Stuart next to a Blenheim bomber

to turn on the British and so aid Japan's cause. To this end it was necessary to have armed guards at readiness In the Squadron Intelligence Summary for the 22nd. The guard consisted of forty Airmen, two Senior Non-Commissioned Officers (NCO) and two Officers in Charge, covering 0730-1930, with a Sikh Regiment taking over at 1930. This security situation also meant that as well as operational flying it was required that patrols be flown in the locality. One such patrol was flown by Stuart on the 14th. Flying Blenheim V5642, Stuart carried out another very low-level recce, this time he hit a signal with the port wing of his aircraft. Although damaged, it was not serious, and he managed to return to base without any problem.

On the 15th and 17th with his crew and Captain Moule, Stuart carried out recces of railways being used by the Japanese. A raid on the aerodrome at Mytikina with three aircraft flying at 12,000ft caused damage to parked enemy aircraft, and the Blenheims encountered some heavy anti-aircraft fire. The rest of the month consisted of various flights between bases.

Flying during August was not easy, as it was the rainy season with heavy rain, hail, and lightning causing problems on the airfields for the ground crews with runways being churned up into mud. The pilots struggled in these conditions and the navigators even more-so, as they were unable to see much due to the thick black storm clouds.

An interesting piece appears in the Squadron Intelligence Summary for 4th September.

Extract from "Operational Information Book" of 1940.

In the air routes books which were issued in this country some two years ago, to pilots flying over routes with which they are not acquainted, the following note appeared underlined where the route passed over delta country (such as the Sunderbans and Irrawaddy delta area). Pilots are especially warned to avoid at all costs, forced landing in Mangrove swamp areas. These areas appear fairly solid from the air, but in actual fact are swamps covered with thick, often impenetrable jungle. Crews of aircraft forced to alight in these areas will find themselves in an extremely hazardous position (that is if they are lucky enough to survive a very dangerous forced landing). The following are some of the difficulties which are likely to be encountered in these areas:

(i) Great difficulty in travelling; through jungle and across broad, frequently swiftly flowing rivers which are more often than not crocodile infested.

(ii) Sparsely populated.

(iii) Deltas have an abundance of snakes, and quite a number of aggressive wild animals.

(iv) Aircraft down in this jungle is quite often invisible from the air thus an air search is of no avail.

Dispersal points were the targets for a raid on 5th September and on the 9th a ship of 3500 tons was sunk in a low-level attack on the docks of Akyab. Thirteen aircraft drawn from 60 and 113 Squadrons took part in this raid with three being lost. The three aircraft lost were one from 60, V5425 which was seen to crash into the sea, the crew being Pilot Officer G Mockridge, Sergeant D Brown and Sergeant D Hall. The other two aircraft lost were from 113, V6507 with pilot Flight Lieutenant O Laone and his crew and V5938 with pilot Sergeant Reid and his crew, with all losing their lives.

By now Stuart was a Flight Commander (OC A Flight. Stuart led three aircraft on a raid to Yenangyuang on the 13th, one fire was started with the mixed bomb load carried. Yenangyuang was strategically important due to its large oil fields. A large proportion of the flying done was relocating from base to forward landing grounds, as had been done in North Africa. Stuart's last operation for September was leading a raid of thirteen aircraft to the railway yard at Mandalay which was heavily defended by anti-aircraft guns. As a Flight Commander Stuart spent much of his time taking out new crews on air tests and training exercises, this filled up the last few days of September. On the 27th Stuart had been made Acting Flight Lieutenant.

Another major problem encountered by all Squadrons operating in Burma was disease and illness. During September it was noted that of the twenty pilots on the strength of 60 Squadron only seven were operationally fit.

By October 1942, the army had been re-equipped, and more troops arrived allowing limited ground offensives in the Arakan. This ended in March the following year as a dismal failure. The Japanese relied heavily on sea and river transport as a means of moving large numbers of men and a vast amount of equipment. The large river-boats could carry 1000 men and as the war progressed, they were all sunk. This was because shipping had been a constant target for the bombers which meant that the Japanese had to rely on other land-based transport with railways being the main alternative.

With the railways being attacked it got to the point where even that became restricted to night movement only. Large locomotive shelters were constructed for protection during the day. The bomber force changed their tactics accordingly, attacking the railways at night and firing R/Ps into the shelters. The Japanese countered this by installing anti-aircraft positions around them for protection. Operations were dictated to a fair extent by the weather.

The nature of the work being done by the bombers meant flying at no more than 100ft above the jungle. Attacking the supply lines was the main type of mission carried out. Having re-located from Asansol to the Advanced

Landing ground at Agatala on the 4th, flying Blenheim Z9828, Stuart took off at 0300 to attack the oilfields at Yenangyuang once more. This raid as conducted by five aircraft of 60 Squadron and five each from 113 and 34 Squadrons. One aircraft returned to base early with engine trouble, but the rest continued to the target. There is scant information about the outcome of this raid apart from the wording of damage being done.

Operating from Agatala again on the 9th, Stuart took off at 0630hrs for a raid on the railway marshalling yards at Ywataung, near Mandalay. This time the five aircraft were joined by six aircraft from 113 and one from 34 Squadron. Once more there is no report to the damage inflicted.

The 12th saw six aircraft from the Squadron carry out a raid on the Japanese barracks at Kelewa with all aircraft returning to base via Jessore after re-fuelling. The Squadron was operational again on the 20th and 25th, the first being to Monywa and the second a strike on Buthedaung. On the 30th Stuart took off in T2291 to conduct a solo offensive reconnaissance in the region of the Chindwin-Homalin area. His aircraft armed with 4x250lb with an 11 second delay, Stuart attacked Japanese trucks. Operational hours flown by Stuart during October added up to 44 hours and 45 minutes. In preparation for the opening of an Officers Mess a meeting was held in the second week of October at which Stuart was made secretary of the mess.

On 3rd and 4th November Stuart undertook photo recce missions of the Homalin area. He spent three hours flying with 10/10ths cloud without incident on the 3rd but on the 4th he nearly hit a mountain. On the 7th he flew with Wing Commander Smyth in a Typsy, he notes in his logbook "Good fun". On the 8th he carried out an offensive photo recce on the Gangaw area and reported that he machine-gunned a Japanese unit using bullocks for transporting of supplies. The docks at Akyab were the target for the 10th when Stuart led eight aircraft on a low-level attack on a 1500-ton ship. On the previous raids during October no mention was made of enemy fighters but on this one they were attacked by a number of them. With a mixed load of 2x250lb General Purpose (GP) bombs and 20x40lb incendiary bombs Stuart flew an offensive recce to the Myitta Valley, bombing and machine-gunning enemy trucks. Although he does not give the actual cause, his port engine was hit by a bullet and put out of action. With a fighter escort, the landing ground at Shwebo was attacked by twelve aircraft from 12000ft. They encountered heavy anti-aircraft fire over the target.

(Authors note, The Typsy referred to is a Typsy Trainer built by the Typsy Light Aircraft Company in Slough).

In December 1942. It was announced by 167 Wing, in the Operations Record Book (ORB) that Flight Lieutenant J S R Muller-Rowland had been awarded the DFC. The Squadron moved from Asansol to Jessore on 21st December. The move was slow due to a lack of transport for the other ranks and ground crews. It was also mentioned that Flight Lieutenant J S R Muller-Rowland had officially ceased to be attached to 45 Squadron and was now posted to 60 Squadron.

There is little to go on in Stuart's logbook, but it does state that he took part in ten raids in January 1943 clocking up 43 hours of operational flying. Much the same for February, with twelve ops undertaken, usually comprising raids on airfields and transport. The exception was on the 12th when he went on a search for an enemy submarine but saw nothing. An entry in Stuart's logbook by Wing Commander D H Banks:

> *'Flight Lieutenant J S Muller-Rowland has*
> *proved himself to be an exceptional Low*
> *Bombing operational pilot.'*

With a total of 344.25 hours of operational flying Stuart was rested with a posting to 152 OTU, at RAF Peshawar dated 17th February. He took part in a raid with 60 Squadron on the 20th and left Dohazari for Peshawar with his crew on 21st. 152 O.T.U. was formed in October 1942 to train pilots out of the Indian E.F.T.S and S.F.T.S. flying a mix of the Blenheim MkI, MkIV and MkV. This posting was to last until 15th May when he was posted to Area HQ Communications Flight.

On 7th June Stuart was promoted to Squadron Leader. The work on the Communications Flight was varied. Stuart was able to fly a large variety of different aircraft. Involving flying all over India He was carrying some very high-profile senior military personnel, flying all over India. On 17th June he took Rear Admiral Read from Bombay to Colombo, picked up four other passengers and flew back to Delhi. Flying Lockheed Hudson MkVI, FK590, Stuart and his crew took General Auchinleck and four other passengers from Delhi to Ambala, collected Wing Commander Russell and then flew on to Chakala where he also picked up General Quinam, flying back to Delhi via Ambala. Another senior officer to be flown by Stuart was Air Marshal Baldwin, taken from Jodhpur to Delhi on 6th August.

Of note, on 25th September Stuart took Major General Orde Wingate from Agra to Gwalior and on to Bangalore, staying over two nights and on to Dum Dum on the 27th. The following day Stuart took Major General Wingate and his party to Imphal. Leaving Imphal on the 29th for Sylhet and returning to Agra via Imphal on the 30th. This was Stuart's last duty with the Communications Flight

211 Squadron Badge

before he was posted to 211 Squadron that was converting to the Bristol Beaufighter.

Stuart joined No 211 Squadron based at Phaphamau on 11th October 1943. This was a very mixed Squadron with personnel from Canada, Australia, and South Africa. 211 was in the process of converting to the Bristol Beaufighter MkX and MkXI, so the first three months of Stuart's flying with them were spent training. Initial training for crews that had not flown the Beaufighter previously was dual on the Bristol Blenheim Mk V also known as the Bisley. In the Bisley, and Blenheims before that, the navigator was situated beside the pilot and carried out some of the cockpit drills as part of his duty. This included monitoring the fuel tanks and transferring fuel when necessary. In the Beaufighter the pilot sat up in the cockpit alone and the navigator was in the rear of the fuselage so all of the jobs that had been done by the navigator fell to the pilot to perform. On 14th October Stuart was fully conversant with the oil, hydraulic and ignition systems along with the cockpit drills on the Beaufighter. Stuart was flying as Officer Commanding B Flight, crewed up with Sergeant Gilley as his navigator.

The Beaufighter was armed with cannon and Rocket Projectiles (RPs). Weapons training consisted of air to ground firing using the cannons at low level and firing the RPs with a 60lb warhead. Army co-operation exercises, where the Squadron would be called upon by the army to support their operations, were an integral part of this.

The first operation with 211 Squadron was on 11th January 1944 when Stuart carried out a "Rhubarb" (usually, where a pair of aircraft fly low level against targets of opportunity, such as river transport, railways, bridges, or road transport). Flying Beaufighter X LZ153 UQ-N, this was to Alon-Yeu Kalewa with 6x 60lb RPs. One hit was seen on the bridge with several near misses with no apparent damage done. On the 15th he undertook "Rhubarb" to Kalewa-Yenanyos, again with 60lb RPs. Following an attack on a bridge, Stuart attacked and damaged three river steamers and an 80ft barge. On the return journey Stuart attacked an oil tank at Yenangyat and oil was seen to be pouring out of it. A couple more tanks were attacked but no results were observed for these. Stuart's aircraft was hit by light anti-aircraft fire, knocking out his port engine but he was able to fly the damaged plane back to base.

The last operation for January took place on the 22nd when four aircraft took off for a "Rhubarb" to attack a bridge over the Meza River with RPs. The centre pillar was struck and damaged. Strafing a locomotive and trucks near Kadu resulted in a large amount of damage being done to the Japanese transport. Some bamboo huts near Manlu provided a target of opportunity for the returning aircraft. Flight Sergeant K J Sealey and Sergeant P G Short were shot down six miles from Indaw, giving off a large cloud of black smoke.

Unlike some of the Squadron operations books the one for 211 shows a monthly summary. As a point of interest, I have included some of these. The figures for January are, in 50 sorties that covered 134 flying hours the Squadron had accounted for:

January	Damaged	Destroyed
Locomotives	9	
Items of rolling stock	33	
Powered craft/River boats	15	1

On the 26th the Squadron moved to Chittagong.

On 7th February, a fighter affiliation exercise took place with Stuart and Sergeant Gilley flying in Beaufighter LZ 131 UQ-W. Things got hotter on the 14th when Stuart took part in a "Rhubarb" to Mandalay-Thazi. Severe damage was done to the bridge at Singaingmyo when girders were torn out by Stuart's RPs. Minan, Myitthi, and a bridge south of Thedaw were also attacked with no visible results of damage. The aircraft strafed a staff car and locomotives with their cannon. Stuart's inner main fuel tank was holed by anti-aircraft fire. On this mission he mentions in his logbook that Flying Officer Sharpe was missing, and Warrant Officer Thomas was wounded.

With LZ131's fuel tank repaired Stuart was one of four aircraft to attack bridges and other railway infra-structure. A bridge at Okshitan was damaged badly with girders, supports and the foundations suffering. Burning camouflage and other debris were seen to be falling from the bridge. Stuart's aircraft was again damaged with bullets through the tail plane. On the return flight he strafed a 15cwt truck at Taungup. A bridge north of Psungdo was targeted on the 22nd when Stuart shot up a locomotive and bus on the return flight having already caused severe damage to the track bed and sending several railway sleepers flying.

On a flight to Feni on the 26th Stuart notes that Flight Sergeant Donaldson went missing. RPs were used against lighters and the jetty Moulmain on the 27th, during this raid Stuart used an RP against a factory and strafed rolling stock and lorries. A signal box was damaged by cannon fire and an 80ft barge was also attacked resulting in black smoke and flames rising to 800ft. The other aircraft attacked buildings round the jetty and rolling stock and goods sheds on the railway.

February was another busy month when in 335 hours of flying the Squadron took part in 71 sorties, which resulted in:

	Destroyed	Damaged or Destroyed
Locomotives		10
Items of rolling stock		50
Motor transport		12
Steamers		4
Rivercraft		55
Enemy aircraft shot down		2

A flight of only 30mins on 3rd March was to attack a dummy airfield using five aircraft. On the 4th the Japanese held village of Lenandaung was attacked with RPs. Huts were set on fire; one MT was destroyed and pontoons over the river were shot up. The 6th was to prove a highly successful day for those involved in an attack on Zayatkwin Aerodrome when Stuart accounted for one Helen (Nakajima Ki 149, heavy bomber) and one Oscar (Nakajima Ki 43, fighter) destroyed, although he in turn was attacked by an Oscar. The six aircraft involved accounted for a total of ten enemy aircraft destroyed for the cost of one of their own, with its pilot, Flying Officer Fuller, being reported as missing.

More damage was done to Stuart's aircraft on a raid to Sacaing-Wuntiio on the 9th. As he was destroying a 3-ton truck, rolling stock, and damaging a railway station at

Ywataung with RPs and cannon fire, Stuart was hit by A/A fire which took out his pitch controls. Two more pilots were shot down with Flying Officer Luing and Warrant Officer Depew missing.

Stuart notes on the 13th that Wing Commander Meacher was awarded the DFC. March was proving to be a busy time for 211 with the losses mounting accordingly. A re-visit to Moulmein on the 14th resulted in one Tug beached and left burning, four lighters being strafed, and one Junk attacked. On this op Flying Officer Cruickshanks went missing.

The tally claimed by Stuart and his navigator showed that he was personally inflicting a lot of damage on the Japanese, but more was to be done.

Stuart carried out a "Rhubarb" on a bridge at Thazi-Yamethin with RPs on the 16th. After attacking the bridge, he strafed the enemy leaving a trail of destruction which comprised one lorry, one car left burning, one locomotive and fifteen trucks shot up. Later that day, taking off at 1827hrs, Stuart was tasked with carrying out a search at sea. Flying alone on this occasion Stuart located one stricken British vessel and sent back the location, this involved a night flight of 5 hours 15 minutes.

The following morning two more aircraft continued the search and located seven lifeboats. Nothing appears in either Stuart's logbook or the Squadron Operations Book to tell us what this was. On the 19th Stuart shared a claim of damaging two locos with another pilot with himself claiming one MT truck destroyed, another two set on fire and a further one damaged. The anti-aircraft fire was heavy and accurate around Meiktila and Amisakan airfields. On the 25th, Stuart attacked 30-40 Sampans, hitting about 20 of these including one large one, and he also attacked three bullock carts. His last op for March was on the 30th to the Bassein area when he sunk one barge, and damaged one tug and four more barges. As the months progressed more work came the way of the Squadron. March was no exception with flying time of 476 hours, 109 sorties were flown which resulted in some major damage to the supplies for the Japanese. The figures for the month were:

	Damaged	Destroyed
Locomotives	12	2
Items of rolling stock	121	25
Rivercraft	277	6
Steamers	25	
Motor transport	Many	Many

The 4th April was when Stuart was awarded a Bar to his D.F.C.

The citation reads:

> *"This gallant officer has participated in very many sorties since being awarded the Distinguished Flying Cross and his continued excellent work has merited high praise. On a recent occasion he led a formation of aircraft detailed to attack targets at Moulmein. The attack was pressed home with great vigour and accuracy. Industrial premises, much rolling stock and a railway installation were bombed with damaging effect; a small pier was set alight, a large barge was hit and other damage was inflicted. In this spirited action, Squadron Leader Muller-Rowland displayed skill, courage and leadership of a high order."*

Stuart was getting into some tight spots. In preparation for a raid on 6th April Stuart flew from his base to an advanced landing ground the previous day. After strafing a 100ft motor vessel (M.V) off Rangoon and leaving it burning Stuart's aircraft was hit by 20mm fire. Struck in the port oil tank, he had to ditch Beaufighter LZ131 UQ-W, in the surf at Teknak. Neither Stuart nor Flight Sergeant Gilley were injured. This was the aircraft Stuart had flown most frequently while he was with 211 Squadron.

After this, April was to prove somewhat lively. The River at Rangoon was the target for the 7th when Stuart attacked three 100- 140ft M.Vs. Again, Stuart's aircraft was damaged by 20mm fire, but this time he managed to return to base. On the 8th a visit to Chenemai resulted in Sergeant Gilley shooting down of a Curtis Hawk being flown by the Siamese and damaging one locomotive and eight trucks at Lanbhun, Stuart made six attacks on these, and on bashas, huts built usually of natural materials, and trucks at Chenemai*. On this raid one of the pilots in Stuart's formation attacked a factory and set it on fire. He shared in the damaging of a locomotive and six railway coaches the following day, also setting fire to a lorry. Flying in very bad weather the trip took over four hours.

Moulmein was a well visited target with another attack on the 16th. With two RPs he hit a 90ft sailing vessel and strafed eight others and some barges. On the 22nd flying LZ527 Stuart, with Flight Sergeant Gilley, left for Maymo. On this occasion he took care of four locomotives and two lorries before being hit by A/A fire which wrecked the hydraulics on the aircraft resulting in him not being able to lower the under carriage. He made it back to base where he made a wheels-up landing. Two of the other aircraft, flown by Flying Officer Lockyer and Warrant Officer O'Mara, returned to base when they failed to

---

* This is how the name appears in the report, but it has not been possible to confirm the location.

contact the rest of the formation due to bad weather. Flight Sergeant Gamlin and Flight Sergeant Lightfoot destroyed and damaged a number of MVs, leaving some burning on the road. The Squadron had undertaken 120 day and 16 night sorties for the month of April.

For his skill as navigator on his many operations 1321801, Flight Sergeant Sidney Ronald Gilley was awarded the DFM on 8th May. Sidney had flown twenty operational sorties and had 101hrs flying time in his logbook. The Air Ministry issued a statement.

> "Flight Sergeant Gilley was the Navigator
> (Wireless) of a Beaufighter which was hit in
> an oil tank on its return from Moulmein.
> During the 25 minutes over enemy territory,
> losing height on one engine, he maintained
> contact with base until the aircraft ditched in
> surf just in our territory. In the next four days
> this NCO carried out three more long-range
> attacks, two of them against airfields in Siam
> and a night attack on shipping off Rangoon.
> In these and two other attacks against
> airfields in which he has been the leading
> navigator, his excellent navigation over
> mountains and at low level has been largely
> responsible for the surprise and success
> achieved. He has completed 20 sorties and
> has shown a very high standard of keenness
> and efficiency. Sorties 20. Flying hours 101hrs
> and 40 mins"

In the London Gazette on 12th May 1944 his citation reads:

> "As navigator, this airman has participated in
> very many sorties and throughout has
> displayed commendable keenness and

efficiency. On one occasion, the aircraft in which he was a member of the crew was severely damaged when hit by enemy fire. Height could not be maintained but the pilot brought the aircraft down onto the sea remarkably close to the shore. Within a few days, Flight Sergeant Gilley had resumed flying and had taken part in two successful attacks on airfields and one on shipping. His accurate navigation over difficult terrain contributed of the success of these sorties".

In view of the above citation, it might well be worth a mention that the role of the navigator was not an easy one. Many of the operations were flown from forward bases which meant moving aircraft in preparation to the following day's ops. Once they had taken off the navigators needed to give the pilots directions to the target, this again was not always straight forward. With sometimes extreme weather conditions and a climb over the mountains which entailed rising, sometimes as high as 11,000ft. Once clear of the mountainous region the aircraft then dropped to low level which on many occasions led to aircraft returning to base with bits of tree hooked up on the wings or underneath. Navigating at these low levels and at speed was made even more difficult by the simple fact that the jungle looked the same wherever you were. With a distinct lack of landmarks, the pilot relied on his navigator to get him to the target and more importantly to get him home.

Flying in Beaufighter NE488 on 10th May, Stuart took off with Warrant Officer Mearns for a raid but trouble with the starboard engine made him abort the mission and feathering the propeller he made a single engine landing back at base. Stuart notes that on this day Flight Sergeant's Davis and Bell along with Warrant Officer

Hall were posted missing, it was later confirmed that all three had been killed. The following day an operation to Tangup-Dalei resulted in Stuart destroying a moving locomotive and forty trucks with his RPs and strafing motor transport.

Mandalay featured highly for the Squadron, on the 13th another visit resulted in two more locomotives being hit and a few trucks destroyed and damaged. The payback for this was Stuart's aircraft receiving damage in the observer's cupola when shot up by light anti-aircraft fire.

Anti-aircraft fire was to cause more problems on the 15th when, during a raid on Hendaza-Prome while attacking two locomotives, two motorcycles and one MT truck, Stuart's aircraft was hit in the port engine by a .5inch bullet. Flying Officer Haakensen's aircraft received damage to one of the wheels and fuselage which meant he had to make a belly landing on return to base. Again, on the 19th the port engine was hit during a raid on MT. On the return, while flying along the Taungun valley, Stuart fired his RPs into the hillside in the hope it might cause a landslide and block the railway and road below. With his cannon's un-serviceable Stuart aborted a raid to Kawlin-Mawlu on the 27th when, after attacking locomotives at Wuntho, he flew on and sighted more rolling stock and locos, but he could do nothing about this as his cannons were jammed. One aircraft had already aborted due to bad weather. The remainder of the aircraft that reached the target successfully destroyed and damaged a substantial amount of rail and river transport. Flight Sergeant Williams's aircraft was severely damaged by anti-aircraft fire and made a belly landing on return to base.

Stuart led a raid on 29th to Hendaza-Prome when a case of friendly fire took place. Warrant Officer Goddard was shot down by P51 Mustangs. The United States Army Air

Force were operating in the area and as a result of mistaken identity a pilot – who had probably had very little training in aircraft recognition – shot down one our aircraft. The USAAF had been working in the northern India-Burma as the American Volunteer group to defend their requirements in the Chinese sector of operations. The USAAF had also been providing logistical support to the British forces in the form of transport aircraft.

Apart from this incident the raid was successful. On leaving the target area the flight left one loco and one car damaged, and a fuel pipeline on fire – Stuart returned to base. His total operational hours by now totalling 151 hours and 35 minutes.

As previously mentioned, the attacks were forcing the Japanese to change their ways of moving supplies. This was now taking place at night a lot more. Consequently, the RAF went on the offensive with more night raids. June 1944 was also to be a busy month, with the Squadron inflicting heavy damages on the Japanese, but their own losses would also mount up. Taking off at 0550hs on the 2nd, Stuart and one other pilot attacked an oil pipeline and strafed and destroyed Sampans at Jimawbi-Leipandan.

The weather was from time to time so bad that flying was impossible, as was the case on the 4th June when Stuart took off at 0238hrs but had to abort due to the weather. An attack on the airfield at Jimawbi on the 6th saw Stuart destroy an enemy fighter on the ground. The next two raids were to Mandalay waterfront, on the 9th seven RPs hit a 100ft barge and the following day an RP on Kaduma and another RP on a 100ft barge. At Mandalay-Shwebo on the 12th, 6 RPs were fired at Kaduma with one locomotive damaged and another destroyed, leaving debris and smoke filling the sky in

Stuart's wake.

As the commander of 211 Squadron, one of the less pleasant tasks Stuart had to perform was writing letters to the families of crews that had been killed or posted missing.

In one incident during the raid on the 12/13th June an aircraft distress signal was picked up and passed on. After there was no reply from the aircraft Flight Lieutenant M J C Haakensen RCAF and his navigator Flight Sergeant A C Fergusson, were posted missing when there was no reply from the aircraft. Stuart's letter to the family was to be the last contact they had until August 1945 when it was discovered the two crew members had been shot down and were prisoners of war. Although not in good shape after their time in the Japanese prison camp, they could nonetheless return to their families at the end of the War.

With engine trouble on the 16th June Stuart did not fly with his comrades in the morning. By the afternoon the plane was ready, and he carried out a sea search, but there are no details of the results of this. On the 20th Tharawaddy-Prome was the target. Of the three aircraft that took off at 0545hrs, Stuart was the only one to reach the target. Pilot Officer MacDonald landed at Chittagong, the weather preventing him from going any further and Flight Sergeant Dickinson returned to base. On reaching the target Stuart hit the pipeline at Sitkwin, Kigon and Thrgon setting it on fire. A locomotive at the railway station at Simiawe presented itself as a good target of opportunity which Stuart promptly destroyed. Stuart landed back at 1026hrs.

One bomber and two M/T trucks were destroyed on a raid to Jimawbi on the morning of the 24th. While Stuart sorted out the airfield, Flight Sergeant Thomson attacked a group of sampans and Flight Sergeant Stayman attacked four water towers at Myttha and then set one truck on fire and damaged two more at Thayetpia. A change of role came on the 26th June when Stuart took part in convoy escort duties.

In his final sortie of the month on the 30th June Stuart achieved a mixed bag. He attacked and set on fire a pipeline five miles north of Minhla; hit a 50ft river craft at Yegin, and a railway shelter with RPs at Theinzeik. These were followed by a truck and buildings and shelters at Martaban-Sittang. A lot of flying time was lost in June due to bad weather, even so, the Squadron still achieved a rather impressive 120 sorties with 404 hours flying time. The bag for the month was:

June	Damaged	Destroyed
Locomotives	5	
Items of rolling stock	69	10
Motor transport	37	25
Steamers	14	1
Rivercraft	231	8

Taking off at 0800hrs on 2nd July, Stuart led an attack on an oil storage tank at Yenanguang which was damaged. Four aircraft took off for the raid, but one returned to base with engine problems. While Stuart concentrated on the oil tank, Pilot Officer McDonald severely damaged a rivercraft and about 20 sampans and 1 MT. Flying Officer Moffat attacked buildings in the area, again causing severe damage.

Rail traffic was once again targeted on the 5th by Stuart while a Japanese troop shelter and accommodation was attacked by the two other pilots. This was to be the pattern for the rest of the month. However, Stuart carried out a couple of solo attacks on the 7th, with good results: two locomotives and several trucks were damaged. At low level with terrible risk to himself and his fellow pilots, Stuart attacked a one-million-gallon fuel storage tank on another raid to Yenanguang- Sedaw on the 20th. The result of this attack could be seen for many miles as the flames and smoke billowed up into the air several hundred feet.

There were fewer operations during August and those that did take place were not as fruitful as in previous months. It was during August that Stuart became the commander of 211 Squadron, although in his logbook it shows that he was O/C of 211 in May, reverting to OC B flight for the next two months. The number of operations undertaken by Stuart dropped this month due to his role as O/C which meant that more of his time was taken up with administrative duties.

Although he flew three operations, on the 2nd, 18th, and 21st August, these followed the same pattern as July. On the 24th while attacking railway targets Stuart's aircraft was hit by light anti-aircraft fire in the port main plane, but he returned to base safely. On 27th August 1944 Stuart led four aircraft on a raid. Two crews saw nothing to attack in the area they were allocated, but Stuart pressed on to his designated area and damaged a steamer and one locomotive. The aircraft flown by Flying Officer Cuddy and his navigator failed to return. The following day Flight Sergeant Begg and his navigator, Flight Sergeant Rowan carried out a search for the aircraft which proved to be unsuccessful.

At the end of the month the ORB shows an explanation on why the Squadron had achieved fewer successes in August:

> *"The month was rather a disappointing one*
> *compared with July and we lost two good*
> *crews, in addition one pilot was wounded. It*

appears that after a successful month against locomotives, a lull next month is inevitable while damaged locomotives are being repaired. Opposition by Light and Heavy Anti-aircraft fire seemed to have been strengthened, probably by the arrival of retreating units from Imphal and Tamu. No airborne opposition was encountered".

On 3rd September Stuart led a raid on the airfield at Hmawbi. Several aircraft on the ground were hit by cannon fire causing substantial damage. On the return Stuart attacked a small fleet of vessels on the river. Warrant Officer Dickinson attacked rivercraft, sinking two and leaving others damaged or burning. The aircraft of Flying Officer Moffat, RCAF had an engine cut out ten miles south of Cox's Bazaar, but he managed to land there safely. Flying Officer Mitchell did not manage to reach the target, returning to base with engine trouble. A raid to Ye, south of Moulmein, was against river traffic and the dock area. The jetty and one barge were damaged followed by a factory and rice mill.

The infamous Burma-Siam railway was a prominent target, one of the main routes for supplies. This is the railway that was built using native labour and prisoners of war. Many allied service men died in its construction and many more suffered the consequences for many years after. On the 9th Stuart led a raid to the railway again leaving a trail of destruction in his wake with 5 locomotives, about 50 railway wagons and 15 passenger coaches in various states of damage. A couple of the pilots also attacked a 1000-ton merchant vessel and an escort vessel leaving both damaged.

The major raid Stuart took part in during September was on the 10th when he led six aircraft. Taking off at 1045hrs they headed for Tenassarim. Once over the target all aircraft attacked using RPs and cannon. The list of successes is impressive, with all nine vessels suffering from their attention. A gunboat was hit, and many coasters were left ablaze while others were damaged, some seriously. As can be seen from the monthly tables, the numerous attacks and losses during early daylight hours meant the Japanese had more and more to rely on night movements of rail traffic in order to make it more difficult for the RAF to attack them.

As a result of this successful attack, more raids were flown in the early hours. On the 15th Stuart took off at 0320hrs to lead another raid of six aircraft on the railway. Significant damage was done with one large locomotive and a medium locomotive hit and four passenger coaches and a truck left burning. Three lorries were also damaged or destroyed and two trains of approximately 30 rolling stock were strafed from end to end with cannon fire.

Although Stuart did not fly on the 17th, a raid was led by Pilot Officer McDonald to docks. Flight Lieutenant Martineau was forced to abort due to the weather and Flying Officer Stayman did not attack. Only Flying Officer Mitchell and Pilot Officer McDonald managed to achieve anything, but they did it in style, setting a wooden barge on fire and damaging or destroying eighteen other rivercraft. Using RPs, they also managed to destroy a tin factory. On the return journey Flying Officer Mitchell was forced to crash land his aircraft near Cox's Bazaar. At 1005hrs Stuart took off to locate the downed aircraft, which he did and stayed in the area to ensure that the two crew members were picked up. Stuart landed back at base at 1455hrs.

In an early morning raid on the 23rd September Stuart and Flight Lieutenant Martineau left behind them three locomotives destroyed and a quantity of rolling stock damaged, all before breakfast!

Stuart ended his tour of operations on the 24th although he did undertake one more raid that afternoon, leading four aircraft to attack road and rail traffic. Pilot Officer Thompson was forced to return to base with an oil leak in the starboard engine. Warrant Officer Arthur Eric England (1270380) and his navigator Warrant Officer Albert Walter Blaxall (1318859) were shot down during the attack. Both were posted as missing and are commemorated on the Singapore War Memorial at Kranji, Singapore.

As this was Stuart's final month in Burma and his last time as O/C 211 Squadron it was a busy time. The monthly summary states that 106 sorties were flown, with 455 flying hours. Recorded strikes for September were:

	Damaged	Destroyed
Locomotives	26	6
Rolling stock	276	Unknown
Water Towers	5	
Steamers	15	
Barges	8	2
Sampans	280	2
MT		
Bullock carts		170
Aircraft (on ground)		1
Other installations (including factories and a rice mill)	18	

The summary goes on to say:

> "A fair month, spoilt by intermittent bad
> weather. The above figures do not bring out

sufficiently an extraordinarily successful strike against shipping in which thirteen vessels were destroyed or damaged. Two aircraft were lost, both at the end of the month. Very few were damaged by enemy aircraft. A few sightings of enemy aircraft were reported".

(Authors note; while the figures are as accurate as they can be it is worth noting that the pilots and navigators could not always see the actual results of their action due to weather, enemy anti-aircraft fire, enemy aircraft or simply because so much was going on. In his book "Towards the Setting Sun" James Bradley states that some allied prisoners of war lost their lives due to the attacks carried out by the pilots of the RAF. This was sadly an inevitable outcome due to the close proximity of the Prisoner of War (POW) camps to the railway and the fact they were in the dense jungle, so the pilots were not to know).

Posted back to Britain Stuart left India from Calcutta. His total operational hours amounted to 658 hours and 20 minutes, with a grand total of flying hours of 1444 hours and 40 minutes.

On his return to Britain Stuart was listed at the No1 Personnel Despatch Centre before being posted to HQ Coastal Command on 20th December 1944. It had been announced on 21st November that Stuart had been awarded the DSO.

It is not known how the death of Eric might have affected Stuart and it was only on his return to England that Stuart learnt of the death of Stanley. Their sister told me that this affected Stuart and possibly led him to greater risks. Like Stanley, Stuart was always striving for perfection in any duty he carried out. The stress of operations over Burma would have been telling on Stuart and to be given the news that his twin had been killed two months before his return would have been a great shock. Whatever the case, Stuart had a duty to do, and he continued to do what was necessary to achieve that goal.

Published in the London Gazette on 17th November 1944 the award was given as;

> *"In recognition of gallantry and devotion to duty in the execution of air operations"*

The Air Ministry Bulletin published in Flight Magazine on 4th January 1945 gave the citation for the award.

> *"Since the award of a Bar to the DFC, Squadron Leader Muller-Rowland has completed many more operational missions. He has consistently shown a fine fighting spirit and flying through adverse weather has on many occasions caused confusion to the enemy's supply lines. He has destroyed three enemy aircraft and damaged others, as well as causing damage to enemy transport and locomotives. Squadron Leader Muller-Rowland's enthusiasm for operational flying, together with his leadership in the face of danger, has contributed much to the success of his Squadron".*

On 28th December Stuart joined Coastal Command Development Unit (C.C.D.U.), his role being with the Air Sea Warfare Development Unit. This unit was operating the Beaufighter as its main aircraft although during this posting Stuart was to fly a variety of other aircraft. These included the Percival Proctor, Hawker Typhoon, Vickers Wellington, Avro Lancaster and Anson, and De Havilland Mosquito. As a sign of things to come Stuart had the opportunity to fly the Prototype Bristol Brigand MA991. A few other types were flown by Stuart while he was with the unit. (*A full list of types that Stuart flew during his career is at Annexe B*). In this role Stuart was to visit many RAF Stations throughout the UK. Just prior to his leaving CCDU, Stuart fractured his left clavicle, this was treated at Chivenor on 17th October 1945. He returned to his unit where he spent the next 14 days on ground duties. Stuart was passed fit to fly again on 29th November.

Stuart was one of the incredible 3% that survived two tours of operations. The many scrapes he had along the way must have had some effect on him. How many of his colleagues did he see go down with the thought that he might be next, or was the idea that so many had, "it won't

DSO, DFC and Bar, 1939-45 Star, Africa Star, Burma Star, Defence Medal and War Medal. Although it is not shown here there should be Oak Leaves on the War Medal for a King's Commendation for Valuable Services in the Air.

happen to me"? It was well known by the family that he was deeply affected by the death of his twin brother Stanley.

Stuart left the unit when he was posted to 248 Squadron. Although on the strength of 248, Stuart was still officially attached to the Naval Tactical Course until the 15th reporting to 248 on 1st November 1945 at Thorney Island. Now with the war over any posting was going to involve mainly training. Although Stuart had already had a little experience on the Mosquito, he now had to familiarise himself with the type operationally. Armed with RPs the Mosquito could pack a punch. Practice firing, navigation exercises and night flying were the subjects to be covered.

Once he had settled in on the Squadron, Stuart's role was to train up new pilots joining the Squadron. Stuart's first flight with 248 was on the 9th for a familiarisation flight. With Warrant Officer Long as navigator Stuart took part in formation flying with the Squadron on the 12th and 14th. The Squadron ORB is rather sparse on information for this period. The only thing of note for December is on the 28th, when Stuart, flying Mosquito RF889 with Flight Lieutenant Ornellas as his navigator, was part of a formation strike on towed targets with RPs.

While still with 248, Stuart attended a course at the US Army Command and General Staff College at Fort Leavenworth, Kansas for four months. Stuart passed out 10th of 233 students and was classed as "Superior", (in RAF classification: "exceptional"). He finished the course on the 25th of June 1946.

On his return to the Squadron, Stuart took part in a wing formation strike on *HMS Vanguard*. The strike was planned for 0545 on 17th July and the briefing took place the evening before, but a final meteorological briefing at 0300hrs on the 17th rescheduled the strike to start at

0515hrs. Stuart remained with the Squadron until August 1946.

A posting to the Bomber Command Instructor School on 28th August led to Stuart being classed as proficient as a low bombing pilot and above average as an instructor on 14th October. Moving on to 36 Squadron, the official date for the posting being 1st October, Stuart's job was to train pilots converting to the Mosquito in its various marks.

This came to an end when Stuart embarked on what was quite likely to be the two most interesting postings of his career. He had obviously proved himself to be a highly capable pilot and leader. Operationally Stuart had certainly gained a wide experience in his RAF career enjoying some remarkably interesting times and surviving a number of extremely close shaves.

CHAPTER 8

Testing Times

As Britain emerged from the Second World War the aviation industry faced new and challenging times. Aircraft had come on leaps and bounds within a few years. At the start of the war all air forces of the world were still operating several biplanes. In some cases, as frontline fighting machines. New, modern aircraft had made their appearance in the 1930s but not always in great enough numbers to meet the need.

As with all wars, necessity bred completely new generations of machines and aircraft, new tactics, and a new breed of men to take steps into this brave new world. In Germany development of aircraft took on a new energy during the war to counter the allied air offensives. The jet engine design of Sir Frank Whittle of the 1930s had become public knowledge pre-war. German scientists had availed themselves of this. With resources made available to them they took giant leaps forward, while Britain was concentrating their efforts on producing conventional aircraft the Germans had managed to create the Messerschmitt 262 jet fighter. This aircraft had entered service in 1944. In some cases, it was deemed too little too late to change the course of the war, but it certainly had a major impact on the allied bomber forces. A few other jet aircraft were to come from the design teams in Germany but none of these were early enough to enter service.

The pulse jet engine had been designed and used in the V1 flying bomb, again this could well have changed the outcome of the war had it come about before the first use in 1944. At Peenemunde, the scientist, Werner von Braun had been working on the development of rockets, the V2 ballistic missile had come from these experiments. Attacks on London proved the ability of the new technologies, a new Blitz had arrived. The rocket powered interceptor, the Messerschmitt 163, had entered service although with a limited flight time and this again made an impact on the allied effort towards the end of the war.

In Britain, the first jet aircraft, the Gloster-Whittle E28/39 first took to the air at Cranwell on the 15th of May 1941 and the Gloster Meteor, Britain's first jet fighter had entered service in 1944. Gloster's rival, De Havilland had the Vampire close to entering service towards the end of the war. The aircraft industry had also been encouraged, with the end of the war in sight, to start planning for the future of air travel. A surplus of war stock and financial constraints initially dictated that aircraft be converted to this purpose or, as in the case of the Avro York and Handley Page Hastings, to make use of parts available from the bombers built by these two companies, the Lancaster and Halifax, respectively.

In some areas the policy makers could not always see where the future lay for the aviation industry and there was, in an age-old manner, a reluctance to change. For those designers and manufacturers involved in the new race for greater speeds and greater capacities the stakes were high. Investment was great, in money, time and manpower. The greatest minds in these companies came up with many innovative ideas to achieve this end.

The Allies had been evaluating captured aircraft all through the war. The Air Fighting Development Unit (AFDU) flew many of these, pitting them against Allied aircraft in mock combat. This gave opportunities to assess the strongest, the weakest, the highs and lows of enemy designs. This evaluation process meant the British industry had a measure of what was required to improve its own products. With the end of the war a wealth of enemy aircraft became available, some of these being relatively common examples of wartime types but alongside these were many prototypes and early production examples of some of the most up to date technology. Vast amounts of design papers reports, and photographs could be assessed by the Allied aircraft industries. Above all the designers themselves were available to the Allies, Britain, and the US. Many of these designers had fled Germany in advance of the Russians and given themselves up, rather than work for the Russians in the Gulags.

The advent of the jet engine meant that speeds previously unheard of were being talked about. The magic point being exceeding the speed of sound. In the UK the two major competitors were Miles Aircraft and De Havilland. Using the knowledge gleaned from captured aircraft designs were being put forward. Miles had been working on their totally revolutionary design, the M52. A long cylindrical fuselage with straight wings, it contained several new inventions that Miles had pioneered. Another innovation, the all-moving tailplane improved upon the fixed tailplane with elevators and was to become a feature on several aircraft in years to come.

The Miles project became a victim of the government when completely out of the blue it was cancelled, with the mock-up being scrapped. Miles was instructed to hand over all the research documents to the Americans giving them the lead they needed to break the sound barrier with the Bell X1. As opposed to a jet this was rocket powered and not capable of taking off from the ground and had to be dropped from an aircraft in flight.

On 14th October 1947 Capt Charles "Chuck" Yeager officially became the first person to fly faster than the speed of sound. This was contested by some as it is thought that the German test pilots had achieved this during the war with some of their experimental aircraft.

Back in Britain, after the cancellation of the M52, the only other contender for the sound barrier at the time was De Havilland. The company had come up with the tail-less DH108 Swallow. The DH108 was initially designed to test the theory of swept wings and to assess performance of this layout. DH were at the time working on the DH 106 Comet airliner which was initially to have been a tailless aircraft and incorporated a 43% swept wing. As this was a relatively new concept there was a need to prove whether this would work. In the light of day with the experience gained from the DH108 the Comet was re-worked to have a tail.

The DH108 was built with a slightly extended cockpit section of the existing DH Vampire with the wings supplemented for short swept back wings, no tail booms, and no tailplane. The design was inspired to a large degree by the Messerschmitt 163 rocket interceptor.

At the forefront of British aviation, Geoffrey De Havilland began his working life with the Royal Aircraft Factory before joining Airco where his designs helped fight the First World War. During the 1920s Airco folded, and Geoffrey formed the De Havilland Aircraft Company. The company became well known for its "Moth" range of aircraft, culminating in the extraordinarily successful DH82 Tiger Moth. This became a standard training aircraft for the RAF, one on which all three Muller-Rowland brothers trained.

Using a winning formula this design could be scaled up, with the company creating a range of twin-engine passenger carrying aircraft, DH84 Dragon and its variants and the four engine DH86 Express. With prizes for aviation DH produced the sleek racer, DH88 Comet which went on to win the Sir Macpherson Robertson prize for Britain to Melbourne. In the 30s the company built the wooden DH91 Albatross which, using the same building techniques, led to the development of one of its most famous aircraft of the Second World War, the DH98 Mosquito. With the advent of the jet age DH developed its Goblin jet engine, which was to power their first jet aircraft, the twin boom DH99/100, Vampire. Its fuselage was built in the same form as the Mosquito with metal wings, boom, and tail. The Vampire's centre section formed the basis for the DH108 Swallow.

Three prototypes of the DH108 were built, the first, TG 283, being a low-speed development aircraft. The first flight of TG283 took place on 15th May 1946. This first flight was followed a month later by the first flight of the second prototype, TG306, was a much more potent high-speed aircraft with a 45% sweep on the wings. Flight testing commenced in TG283 with Geoffrey De Havilland Jnr, company chief test pilot and son of Sir Geoffrey De Havilland at the controls.

The second aircraft, the TG 306, joined the test programme in August. Geoffrey De Havilland continued to put the little aircraft through its paces. In early September Geoffrey achieved 630 miles per hour, leading to the decision to have an attempt at breaking the world speed record. This was unfortunately to have catastrophic consequences on 27th September 1946. While flying over the Thames Estuary the aircraft went into a dive and broke up in mid-air. The wrecked aircraft coming down into the water. Geoffrey De Havilland's body was washed ashore near Whitstable a few days later. Witnesses at the time recall hearing a loud bang; whether this was Geoffrey breaking the sound barrier or whether this was just the sound of the aircraft breaking up will never be known.

With the demise of Geoffrey, the well-known wartime pilot, Group Captain John "Cats eyes" Cunningham, CBE, DSO and 2 Bars, DFC and Bar, Air Efficiency Medal, took on the role of chief test pilot for De Havilland. In September 1948, flying VW120, the third prototype, with a cleaned-up air frame, longer, pointed nose and a Martin-Baker ejection seat was built. Cunningham and his colleague, test pilot John Derry carried out flights that set new speed records with the little aircraft which now had an up rated De Havilland goblin engine.

A few firsts: on 9th September 1948, taking the 108 to 40,000 feet John Derry became the first pilot in Britain to fly faster than the speed of sound and the 108 became the first British aircraft to fly faster than the speed of sound, albeit in a fast dive as opposed to level flight. The difference with this flight and that of Chuck Jaeger was that Jaeger's aircraft was released from a bomber in flight whereas the 108 took off under its own propulsion. Joining the Aerodynamic flight at Farnborough, this aircraft, joined its stablemate, the second prototype, TG283 and went on to be used in several tests to discover the characteristics of small tail-less aircraft.

Stuart Muller-Rowland's successor at Farnborough, Squadron Leader George Eric "Jumbo" Genders, took the TG283 out in May of 1950 only for that aircraft to suffer the same problems as Stuart experienced. Although Jumbo tried to bale out, his parachute got caught up and he also died because of this same little aircraft.

The loss of these aircraft was a huge blow to the British aviation industry, three very experienced test pilots died while trying to tame it. On the other hand, a significant lesson was learnt about the swept wing design which became a major element on De Havilland's later DH Comet airliner. The Comet was to become the world's first jet airliner to enter service. A foot note to this is that two years to the day of the breaking of the sound barrier by John Derry, he was flying another of De Havilland's prototypes, the DH110, at the Farnborough Airshow. After making a high-speed entry and breaking the sound barrier the aircraft broke up, killing John and his navigator, Tony Richards. This is the worst airshow disaster in British history to date. Twenty-nine spectators died and many more were injured as the aircraft debris fell into the crowd.

With the types of jet aircraft, it was no longer a case of a pilot jumping in and having a go. Financially the risks were too great as were the risks to the test pilots. The complexity of the jets was so much greater than the earlier piston engine aircraft. The test pilots needed a much more in-depth knowledge of the technology involved. It was the job of the principal Scientific Officer at ETPS to teach the students about aerodynamic stability and the relevant mathematics.

The test pilot's job sounds very daring, which of course it was, but most of the flying was of a very mundane nature. Apart from the testing of jet aircraft many new features were being developed. To prove the concept and viability of new systems, conventional aircraft were used as test beds. Electrically or hydraulically powered control systems were being developed and improved upon for driving the flaps, elevators, and trim tabs. All of these innovations were necessary for the ability of the pilots to fly the new breeds of aircraft. It was difficult enough for the pilots to operate these systems in conventional aircraft which had been growing ever faster and more complex during the war years. Now with the greater speeds, the reactions of the pilot and the manoeuvrability of the new generation of aircraft would become vital. The manual, mechanically operated systems would not be quick enough.

Wing planforms* was a major factor in the new breed of aircraft. Thinner wings to increase the airflow and reduce drag had come about much earlier with the laminar flow wings. To reduce buffeting at high speed it was necessary to have a sweep on the wings, this was trialled with various degrees of sweep to find the ultimate angle. Much later the swing or variable incidence wing was developed to enable greater stability in low and high-speed flight and high and low-level flight, this made an aircraft much more adaptable for use in different roles. Another concept being developed at the time was the delta wing. All of these features were later incorporated into production aircraft, both military and civil. It was critical to get a reliable view of the effects of airflow below and above the wing. The method for doing this was relatively simple. By fixing tufts of wool to the wing surface the airflow could be observed by camera either mounted on the aircraft or operated by an observer in another aircraft flying alongside. Similarly, smoke released from another aircraft could be observed in the same manner. Other test pilots would fly the spotting aircraft with members of the scientific branch on board to observe and record the results.

In the case of the high-speed jets, aerodynamic stability was still an unknown quantity. Aerodynamic drag was induced as the speed of sound was approached, which meant the designers needed to explore the character-istics of these new types of wing. At the time, the technology did not exist to be able to record, on the ground, what was happening in the air. The only way to

---

* The wing planform is the silhouette of the wing when viewed from above or below.

record this was the test pilot writing down what he observed and passing this on to the designers.

It is now a matter of fact that many people jump on board aircraft, particularly jets and fly all over the world without giving a second thought to the fact that it was the test pilots of the aircraft manufacturers and those research test pilots at Farnborough that did all the initial flying in the early jets. It did not matter whether these were the most advanced designs for military use or for the civil market. The proximity for both was close when learning handling characteristics and new designs and ideas of either. The work carried out in the design of the wings for the DH108, DH110, and the DH Comet is still relevant today with the plant at Hatfield building wings for the Airbus Company.

Test flying in the 1950s was a very risky business to be in. Entirely new concepts, designs, and engines were being tested, and engines were not always as reliable as one would hope. These test pilots would literally be learning on the job, there were no textbooks to read, the only pilot notes were those drawn up by themselves or by their colleagues. In a day when computer programmes did not exist to test out the theories of high-speed flight and the effects of exceeding the speed of sound these pilots were quite often flying into the unknown daily. Test pilots still exist and still carry out remarkable work but well before the prototypes are even built the designs have been scrutinised in a way that was never dreamt of in the 1950s.

Back Row

F/Lt G.W.	F/Lt L.W.	F/Lt J.R.	F/Lt D.G.	S/Ldr R.A.	S/Ldr R.G.	F/Lt W.H.	S/Ldr A.	F/Lt L.S.	F/Lt V.R.L.	S/Ldr C.E.	F/Lt J.S.R.		F/Lt G. J.	F/Lt D.V.
Johnson	Stark	Stoop	McCall	Watts	Woodman	Scott	Tooth	Lumsdaine	Evans	De Voigne	Muller-Rowland		Chandler	Sutton
DFC	DFC				DSO DFC	DFC	DFC	DFC		DSO DFC	DSO DFC			

Middle Row

F/LtR.L.	F/LtD.A.	S/LdrR.W.	F/LtA.E.	F/LtN.F.	LtA.C.	Lt(A I.M.	LtCdrH.E.	LtCdr(E)G.F	.LtCdrW.F.	Lt(A)R.M.	Lt(A)R.H	LtCdr(E P.	MrT.W.	S/LdrD.J.	F/Lt V.B.	F/Lt G.	F/Lt S.
Duncan	Dunlop	Whittome	Callard	Harrison	Lindsay	Maclachan	Hoener	Hawkes		Krantz	Crossley	Reynolds	Richmond	Brook-Smith	Williams	Carson	Banner	McCreith
AFC	DSO DFC	DSO DFC	DFC	DSO	DSC		NC DFC			DSC		DSC		DSO DFC		DFC	AFC
			SAAF	RN	RN	USN		RN		USN							

Front Row

Mr J.	F/O L.N.	F/Lt K.E.	F/Lt F.R.	S/Ldr K.J.	Commander F.M.A.	Gp Capt S.R	Mr G. Maclaren	S/Ldr R.E	S/Ldr E.N.M.	S/Ldr E.J.	F/Lt P.F.	F/Lt R.E.
Lawford	Flower	Walters	Arnold	Sewell	Torrens-Spence	Ubee	Humphreys	Havercroft	Sparks	Watts	Wingate	Humphreys
B.Sc.	DFC	AFC		AFC DFM	DSO DSC AFC	AFC	B.Sc.,A.INST.P.,		DFC	MBE	DFC	
(Tech)	(Times Offr)	(QFI)	(Adj Flying)	(Tutor Flying)	RN	The	A.F.R.Ae.S	(Tutor Flying)	(Tutor Flying)	(CTO)	(QFI)	(Eng Offr)
					(OC Flying)	Commandant	(CTI)					

164

CHAPTER 9

The Fateful Day

On 2nd March 1947 Stuart received his posting to The Empire Test Pilots School at RAF Cranfield. Reporting on 29th March, Stuart joined No 6 Course. With thirty-four students, the course was mixed, with pilots from Australia, South Africa, Canada, and the US Navy. The British contingent was taken from all RAF Commands and the Royal Navy. By the nature of the school the types of aircraft flown were very varied: training aircraft, high performance single engine aircraft such as the Seafire 47, and multi engine bombers. Aerobatics were to play a large part in Stuart's training, initially in the NA Harvard MkII and then the more powerful aircraft.

It was here that Stuart first gained experience in jet aircraft, his first flight being in the Gloster Meteor MkIII EE398 on 29th April 1947. At a time of great leaps forward in aviation, test pilots were flying several different types of aircraft. August proved to be a difficult month at ETPS when the move was made to Farnborough, as RAF Cranfield was closing. The final flight by ETPS being made on the 29th. Between the 25th and 28th November students on the course went on visits to some of the aircraft manufacturers: Bristol Aero Co at Filton, Gloster Aircraft at Hucclecote, Westland Aircraft at Yeovilton and the propeller manufacturer, Rotol Ltd at Gloucester, and Moreton Valance. This was to enable the students to see at first hand the developments being made in aircraft. At Filton they had a look at the large new hangar that housed the large Brabazon airliner.

Stuart in uniform

Another opportunity for visits came on the 15th to 18th December when they went to A V Roe and CO, Manchester, Rolls Royce Engines in Derby and Saunders Roe at Cowes on the Isle of Wight. The end of course dinner had been held on 12th December 1947 with awards being given, and speeches made by representatives of the aircraft industry and RAF Senior Officers. The course ended on the 19th. Along with Stuart, Squadron Leader R W Whittome OBE DFC, Squadron Leader L C C Le Vigne DSO DFC, Flight Lieutenant G J Chandler, Flight Lieutenant C L Brooks, Flight Lieutenant G Banner DFC and Lieutenant R H Reynolds DSC RN, all went on to the Experimental Flying Department at Farnborough. With the remainder going to Aeroplane and Armament Experimental Establishment (A&AEE), RAF Boscombe Down, Wiltshire, Marine Aircraft Experimental Establishment (MAEE), RAF Felixstowe, Suffolk, *HMS Peregrine*, Royal Naval Air Station (RNAS) Ford, Sussex, and *HMS Daedelus*, Lee on Solent, Hampshire. The overseas graduates returned home.

Once he had completed his course, Stuart joined the Aerodynamic Flight at Farnborough. The job entailed a wide range of testing on prototypes, establishing behaviours of different types of wings and observing the flow of air over the aircraft. Much of the flying was of a very mundane nature but the job also entailed some exciting moments in the much faster jet aircraft. A test pilot needed to be quick thinking with fast reactions to ensure that should a problem occur he could respond to it. The pilot also had to make notes of his findings, although very often this was done by crew members, and in the larger aircraft there would often be members of the technical sections or from other trades doing this. On single seat aircraft it was down to the pilot with a notepad strapped to his leg!

The first British jet-propelled aircraft had only flown a few years previously and now the goal was to break the sound barrier. Britain, just prior to 1948 was leading the world and Martin Baker and De Havilland were building aircraft with this aim in mind. At speeds approaching the sound barrier several different aspects with the wing design and air flow over the wings created buffeting and stability problems. To test these handling characteristics the RAE used Gloster Meteors and De Havilland Vampires. Soon after arriving at Farnborough, Stuart began investigating the effects of high-altitude flight in a Meteor. The Meteor was capable of speeds quite close to the sound barrier, so this made it an ideal platform from which to conduct trials and evaluate the effects of high mach numbers. Some of the Meteors on charge at Royal Aircraft Establishment (RAE), were twin seat so it was possible for an observer to be a passenger. Quite often these observers were civilian scientists working in the research department.

The commander of the Aerodynamic Flight when Stuart arrived at Farnborough was Lieutenant Commander Eric 'Winkle' Brown. "Winkle" Brown holds the world record at 487 different types of aircraft flown, and of these he flew many different marks and other aircraft of the same type. Winkle left the Flight in late 1949 leaving the position open for Stuart to take command.

Stuart's logbook for the period August 1948-February 1950 does not appear to exist; if it does, the family do not know where it might be. I have, to the best of my ability re-constructed it from the flight logs of Farnborough. (Annexe C)

Stuart, with his knowledge and experience was selected by Headquarters, Ministry of Supply to tour the Experimental Establishments of the United States Air Force.

During his time at Farnborough, Stuart became a close friend of Squadron Leader (later Group Captain) Johnny Kent, a former Battle of Britain pilot. Johnny was the Chief Test Pilot. This friendship led to Johnny naming his first child Stuart. Johnny had completed a tour at Farnborough in the late 1930s. His role included that of test pilot with the Experimental Flight of the Royal Aircraft Establishment.

In his book "One of The Few" he writes.

> During my second tour of duty at Farnborough, a time which coincided with what was the most dangerous period of its history. We had suffered a number of casualties as had the Empire Test Pilots School. Our first loss, which we could ill afford, was that of Squadron Leader Wittome who, having miraculously survived a very nasty crash in a Meteor, lost his life in a Spitfire shortly afterwards. Aside from our thus losing a very nice person we also lost an out-standing test pilot who had come top of the course at the ETPS.

(Author: this was No 6 course, the same one that Stuart attended).

Second to Wittome only by a hairsbreadth at ETPS was Squadron Leader Stewart (sic) Muller-Rowland, the youngest of three brothers all of whom distinguished themselves during the war. When Brown* was posted back to Naval duties, Muller-Rowland succeeded him as Flight Commander and an extremely efficient one he was too.

(*Author: Lieutenant Commander Eric Brown).

At this period, the Delta configuration was undergoing investigation and development and two designs were in progress. One, the Avro 707, had made a number of flights at Farnborough piloted by the firm's test pilot, Red Essler, it crashed some miles from the airfield killing the pilot. The second design was being built by Boulton and Paul to RAE specifications and the initial flight trials were to be conducted by the RAE test pilots, which meant that I should make the first flight.

Wind tunnel stability tests had been anything but encouraging and, in view of this and my slight experience of the 108 (De Haviland), I was not perhaps, as enthusiastic as I might have been. On the other hand, Muller-Rowland was just itching to get his hands on it, but still it was my responsibility.

We discussed this at length one day and,

although we could both see and appreciate the other's point of view, it was obvious that he would be very disappointed if he did not make the first flight. I made it clear that I did not wish to steal his thunder, but it was a risky thing and I felt that it was my duty to make the first flight.

He quite saw my argument, but he said: 'I understand but I do not think that you should automatically take on every risky job just because you are Chief Test Pilot although in fact, this thing I am flying this afternoon is far more dangerous than the Delta.'

We were obviously not getting anywhere so I said: 'OK, we'll have another talk about it nearer the time and maybe we can thrash out something suitable to both of us.' Twenty minutes later he was dead.

I watched him take off in the Swallow (DH108) and climb away to the north-east. It seemed no time at all before I had a telephone call telling me that that the aircraft had been seen coming out of cloud in pieces, and that the pilot's body had been found in the wreckage. This loss was a frightening blow and it affected everybody, even those who had not even known him personally, while to me, with the memory of our last conversation, it came as a bitter blow.

As it happened, Johnny Kent did not get to fly the Delta as it arrived at Farnborough just as he was leaving for an exchange visit to the US.

At 1115hrs on 15th February 1950, Stuart took off from Farnborough in DH108 Swallow VW120. The purpose of the flight was to establish transitional aspects of sub-sonic to transonic flight. Having reached a height of about 35,000 feet Stuart put the aircraft into a dive.

It had already been discovered that the Swallow entered violent oscillations when approaching the speed of sound. Severe porpoising threw the pilot about in the cockpit. Eric Brown describes in his book "Wings on my Sleeve" that in one minute his head hit his chest and the next his head had been thrown backwards. This later helped to establish the cause of Geoffrey De Haviland's death in 1946.

(Authors note; Porpoising is the motion of the nose of the aircraft suddenly diving and then just as suddenly rising up, while going forward, getting the name from the motion of a porpoise or dolphin).

The initial Air Accident Investigation gave rise to the feeling that there was a problem with the aircraft's oxygen supply. An inquest was opened two days later. At the inquest into Stuart's death the coroner's report stated that the cause of death was a broken neck. With Stuart already dead, at 27,000 feet the aircraft was out of control. In this uncontrolled state the Swallow plummeted towards the ground. A few witnesses recalled hearing a loud bang which at the time was thought to be the aircraft breaking the sound barrier but was later found to be from the aircraft breaking up.

Wreckage was spread over a wide area, with most of the wreckage coming down at Little Brickhill near Bletchley. Buckinghamshire. The cockpit came to earth at Bow Brickhill Church and Stuart's body was found in Sandy Lane. A quantity of smaller parts of the aircraft were found some distance away from the main wreckage.

Although the Swallow had by this time been made public and been exhibited at the Farnborough Air Show it was still regarded as secret, and only limited information about the aircraft had been released to the press. Many of the innovations incorporated in it were still relatively new. It was because of this that the local Police secured the site to avoid onlookers gathering and souvenir hunters taking pieces from the crash site.

I have not established how Daisy received the news of Stuart's death but the first thing that Joan, Stuart's sister knew of this was when her husband, Richard rushed home from work with a copy of the Evening Standard. The "Standard", carried a report about the crash that day. Richard had seen the headline on the paper that one of his patients had in his surgery. Joan was at home with her month-old daughter Carolyn and two-year-old son, Mike. The news was in the public domain before the whole family had been told.

Proof, if it was needed, as to the professionalism, popularity, and esteem Stuart was held in is the letters that Daisy received following his death. The first letter was from Hatfield Aerodrome, dated 16th February 1950, from Geoffrey de Havilland, Snr, of De Havilland Aircraft.

> Dear Mrs Muller-Rowland,
>
> The news of the tragic accident to your son came as a great shock. On such occasions as these words seem inadequate to express our feelings. I can, to some extent, share your sorrow and understand what it means to you because of my son's fatal accident in a similar machine some years ago.
>
> Many modifications were then made in the new model, and it had done a great deal of

highspeed work. We were very optimistic
that all previous troubles had been
eliminated, but this high-speed research
must always carry risk.

I can only send my deep and sincere
sympathy to you in your tragic loss.

Letters from many people at RAE Farnborough, the
Ministry of Supply, and the Air Ministry all expressed
sympathy and gave glowing reports of Stuart's achievements. A letter from someone virtually unknown to
Daisy was from Lieutenant Colonel TA Wainwright RA.
Wainwright first met Stuart in Burma in 1942, and they
worked together on many occasions, with Stuart flying
him to many different locations, so he appears in Stuart's
logbook. Wainwright had visited Stuart when he was in
hospital at Maymyo in March/April 1942. Wainwright
had written to Daisy to reassure her that Stuart was "fine
and dandy". Wainwright goes on to mention another
meeting they had, soon after Stuart took his first
command, a rocket equipped Beaufighter Squadron.
Wainwright says that Stuart took him to see his new toys,
of which he was excited. He then goes on to say, "…with
which he was [to] later [fly] to such magnificent effect in
Burma", Wainwright also says that he often referred to
the "brave youngster" in letters.

Lieutenant Commander Peter Twiss, OBE, DSC and Bar,
chief test pilot for Fairey Aviation, was among the
wartime flyers that wrote to Daisy. Daisy raised the
question of the minimal pay that test pilots received in a
letter to the Daily Express. This letter prompted Group
Captain Hugh "Cocky" Dundas, DSO, DFC, aviation
correspondent to the Daily and Sunday Express, to write
an article about test pilots in general. Dundas was an
ex-Battle of Britain pilot. Many private letters flooded in

which just goes to show the impression Stuart had made. Many other letters appear in Daisy' cuttings book, from the Air Ministry, Ministry of Supply and RAE Farnborough, plus many from private individuals. (*Authors note, Sir Hugh Dundas, CBE, DSO and Bar, DFC. Hugh Dundas was a well-respected fighter pilot and veteran of the Battle of Britain*).

In his book Johnny Kent goes on to say:

> The post of Flight Commander thus left vacant had to be filled by someone upon whom we could rely and whom we knew had the requisite experience and ability. "Jumbo" Genders[1] had been posted away a few months previously and, in the normal course of events, would not have been allowed to come back to experimental flying until he had completed at least one tour on normal RAF duties. In view of the unusual situation, however, I did manage to have an exception made and Jumbo returned to us and took over the Aerodynamics Flight.
>
> Three 108s were built in all, the first was basically a Vampire with a special swept wing and fixed slats but was not capable of any great speed. The other two were very much cleaned up and John Derry had become the first Briton to exceed the speed of sound in a British aircraft whilst flying the same machine in which Stewart Muller-Rowland was later killed. Previously Geoffrey De Haviland himself had been killed in the other high-speed model when it disintegrated over the Thames Estuary.

Within a month of taking over the Flight, Jumbo went off in the remaining 'slow' 108 to carry out some stalling tests. The next I heard was that the machine had crashed some ten miles from the airfield. Jumbo had baled out but was too low for his parachute to save him. Progress must go on and research continue to enable it to do so, but I have often felt that the price we pay is too high and in the loss of these quite outstanding young men I feel it was much too high.

As can be seen from this account, which gives an indication of the dangers these men faced, Stuart's death was not uncommon among this small elite of test pilots.

The funeral for Squadron Leader John Stuart Rowland Muller-Rowland DSO, DFC, and Bar, took place at St Mary's Church, Horsell on Monday 20th February 1950, when he was interred in the family vault. The chosen hymn was O Valiant Hearts.

Stuart had amassed a total of 2380 hours and 55 minutes flying time. He had also achieved 10 hours and 55 minutes on the Swallow (DH108). It is rather ironic that Stuart, with all his experience did not have a private pilot's licence until 27th June 1949 when his was granted.

An interesting footnote to Stuart's story is that David Lean, film producer, read the obituary in the papers. This was the inspiration for the film "Sound Barrier" which was released in 1954.

1. 'Jumbo' Genders

The successor of to the post of C/O Aerodynamic Flight was Squadron Leader George Eric Clifford 'Jumbo' Genders. Born in Doncaster in 1920, George joined the RAFVR. After training he embarked with 73 Squadron to sail to the West Coast of Africa. He was flying Hawker Hurricanes over Egypt before being posted to 33 Squadron in Greece in 1941. George was awarded the DFM in April 1942 and commissioned in May of the same year. After an illustrious wartime combat career including testing a variety of aircraft while posted to 103 MU, he went to the Empire Test Pilots School at Cranfield in January 1946 and joined the Aerodynamic Flight at Farnborough. Here he was one of the pilots assigned to test the DH108. George was awarded the AFC in the New Year Honours of 1949 for his services to testing aircraft. With the death of John Muller-Rowland, George succeeded him as C/O of the Aerodynamic Flight on 14th March 1950. Flying DH108 TG 283 on 1st May he got into trouble over Hartley Wintney. With the aircraft toppling out of the sky, George attempted to bail out at 200ft. George's parachute had got hooked up on the aircraft and he was seen by a witness to be still attached to the aircraft as it crashed to the ground.

From the Family 3

August 22nd, 1948. It is my fifth birthday, and I am spending it at my maternal grandmother's house in Middleton-on-Sea in Sussex. It is a glorious summer's day with a cobalt blue sky. Parked in the drive is a sports car. It belongs to my Uncle Stuart, who is visiting his mother for the weekend. He lifts me up so that I can sit on the bonnet. I am in seventh heaven. It is one of my earliest memories. At five I was not quite old enough yet to hero worship my uncle, but it is all that remains for me of him and his two brothers. It was dangerous work, and he acknowledged this by committing himself to stay single while he was doing it. He was right because 18 months after that summer Sunday he was dead. They were three boys with a passion for flying that seems to have known no bounds, a passion that they presumably shared with many of 'the few'. It has been said of them that into their short lives they packed more than many who live to old age.

Richard Mason.

I too remember Stuart very well: his visits to our home in Chobham often in uniform on his way home from Farnborough; his cheerfulness; his sense of fun and his generosity. He often brought us presents which was a rare occurrence in those days.

Remembered with warmth and affection by his eldest niece.

Jane Hoyle (nee Mason).

CHAPTER 10

Memorials

Eric is commemorated on The Malta Memorial Panel 6, Column 2. Eric's next of kin details his father as John Muller-Rowland and mother Daisy of Guildford, Surrey. Eric is also remembered on the Uppingham School War Memorial.

Stanley is commemorated on panel 201 of the Royal Air Force Memorial at Runnymede and the Uppingham School War Memorial. Stanley is also commemorated on the memorial to all members of the North Coates Strike Wing at the Town Hall in Cleethorpes, Lincolnshire.

Alan Kendall is commemorated on Panel 207 of the Runnymede Memorial. In the years following the Second World War, Williams Deacon's Bank was taken over by the National Westminster. At the office in Hardman Boulevard, Manchester is the Bank Memorial, Alan's name is listed there.

Ernest William Alexander is commemorated on Panel 7, Column 1 of The Malta War Memorial.

Runnymede Memorial. It was on Saturday 17th October 1953 that the Imperial War Graves Commission held the unveiling of The Royal Air Force Memorial by Her Majesty the Queen. The wording of the official Order of Service:

The Runnymede Memorial

Has been built by the Imperial War Graves Commission in memory of 20,455 airmen who gave their lives in the 1939-1945 War and have no known graves. They died for freedom in raid and sortie over the British Isles and the lands and seas of Northern and Western Europe.

After the service and General Salute wreaths were laid, the Queen, followed by the Duke of Edinburgh and the Duke of Gloucester (President of the Imperial War Graves Commission). These were then followed by:

The Secretary of State for Air, and the High Commissioners of, South Africa, Australia, New Zealand, Pakistan, Canada, and India. The Chief of the Air Staff, and finally as the memorial is in the district of Egham, the Chairman of Egham Urban District Council.

A Service of Remembrance was held at Uppingham on Saturday 11th November 1950. This was attended by Daisy, who by this time had lost all three of her sons. The service opened with The National Anthem and the following prayer.

Brethren, we are met together in the presence of Almighty God, in this chapel where they worshipped, to do honour to the memory of those former members of the School who gave their lives in the last war; and to give thanks for their devotion and self-sacrifice.

Rest eternal grant unto them, O Lord, and let Light perpetual shine upon them.

In the Church of England Chapel at Royal Air Force North Coates, Lincolnshire, the RAF Station Memorial was unveiled by the Station Commander Group Captain F J St G Braithwaite, OBE, on 13th August 1944 to commemorate the airmen flying from North Coates who lost their lives. It is possible, that Alan Kendall attended this ceremony, as this was in August, and he was not killed until October that year. Stanley had not yet joined the squadron. When RAF North Coates closed, the Memorial was moved to St Nicholas Church, North Coates. Alan and Stanley are just two of the five hundred and twenty-one names on this memorial.

The Royal Air Force Memorial Flight, formerly The Battle of Britain Memorial Flight exists as a flying memorial to all those that served and lost their lives in the Royal Air Force. Based at Coningsby, Lincolnshire, they operate Britain's only airworthy Lancaster Bomber, six Spitfires, two Hurricanes and a Douglas Dakota. With only a skeleton full-time staff, the flight is operated by volunteers from the various trades within the RAF.

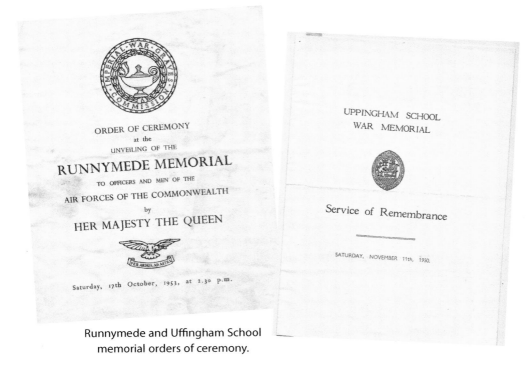

Runnymede and Uffingham School
memorial orders of ceremony.

From the Family 4

Some personal comments from nephews and nieces.

Our grandmother had lost all three sons before they were thirty and with them died the Muller-Rowland name. Whenever people die young, we are left with the question of what they might have been, we only know what they were, and this is their story. Only one of Daisy's grandchildren was born before Stanley was killed, and none of us before Eric's death. Although, those of us born before Stuart was killed have vague memories of him, but we never got to know him.

Richard

They were iconic figures who symbolised the bravery shown by so many young men of their generation, but the difference for us, is that they were "our" heroes, and therefore their achievements and deaths resonate so much with us. It is truly relevant that we are all still absorbed by this story now, some seventy to eighty years after their deaths.

David

I think the three brothers, our uncles, were ordinary people who did extraordinary things in extraordinary times at great sacrifice to themselves and their family. We feel great pride but also great sadness at the loss of such young lives and that we never knew them.

Judy

CHAPTER 11

On Reflection

An incredible family. Hans worked hard to get where he did. They were well travelled, an opportunity that not many had, although this was related to work. Hans had built up a vast array of contacts and was a well-respected member of the community. The process for him to become a British citizen was quite a drawn out one. Not only did he need referees, but these were also then checked out by the police who had to verify those people. The file at the National Archives is quite a size with the various correspondence relating to this.

It is hard for us to contemplate what it must have been like for the "boy's" mother and sisters with two brothers being killed during the war and then Stuart being killed later.

While researching and writing this book I had the privilege of handling some extremely interesting and important documents relating to these three, brave, popular, and highly respected brothers. Without the support of their youngest sister and the nephews and nieces I would not have been able to bring the book to life. As with my first book, I have immersed myself in it to such a way that although they died before I was born, I feel as though I somehow knew them.

To repeat the first three words of this chapter, "An incredible family". It was not just Eric, Stuart, and Stanley that sacrificed so much. Daisy played her part at home, losing two of her sons during the war, and the third later. Joy gave her time nursing and Joan being a doctor both serving overseas. Too young to serve, Wendy was whisked off to Australia, for the safety it could offer, returning after the war. We can only imagine what it must have been like for Wendy to return to her mother with two brothers killed. The shock of coming home to the deprivations of austerity and rationing must have taken a lot of getting used to. Life had changed dramatically in the time she had been gone. We should also not forget the part that Joy and Joan's husbands played, with Richard and Reginald both serving in the army, and Daisy's nephew, Frank who had been killed in Tunisia. The others we should think about are the two crew members who died with Eric and Stanley, Ernest Alexander, and Alan Kendall: their families suffered the same. Many more gave their lives alongside these people mentioned in this book, and many served with great devotion to keep these men in the air to continue the struggle against tyranny.

A late development in the writing of this book came about through one of the Muller-Rowland, nephews, John who lives in Canada. As I mentioned Leslie, Alan Kendall's niece lives in Toronto, and John wanted to be in touch with her, so now the two families are in contact, nearly seventy-seven years after their uncles lost their lives.

It has been suggested by the family that there could be enough material for a book on the women of the family, Joan has written her memoirs, but these have not been published.

The last word:

Three remarkable brothers, they followed a path that they might otherwise not have taken had the war not intervened. They, like many of their generation got on with it. I think you the reader would agree that Eric, Stuart, and Stanley showed exceptional leadership qualities, and devotion to duty, balanced with being very likeable fellows. I know from the correspondence from the family that they were heroes to them, although most of the nieces and nephews had not been born during the brothers' lifetimes. This is how legends are remembered. I started as a complete outsider and now feel that I am part of the story. I am proud to have been able to bring this piece of history out for the world to see and hope that their story will not be forgotten.

Eric, Stuart, and Stanley, we salute you.

ANNEX A

Aircraft flown by Stanley Muller-Rowland

During his career Stanley flew a number of types of aircraft. Although he was a bomber pilot on twin engine aircraft, he did get to fly a few single engine types.

1. DH82 Tiger Moth
2. Airspeed Oxford
3. Avro Anson
4. Bristol Beaufort
5. Handley Page Hampden
6. Bristol Blenheim
7. Bristol Beaufighter
8. North American Harvard
9. Hawker Hurricane
10. Supermarine Spitfire
11. Fairey Gordon
12. Fairchild Argus
13. Percival Proctor
14. Vickers Wellington
15. Boulton Paul Defiant
16. Miles Magister

Aircraft flown by John Stuart Muller-Rowland during his remarkable career as a pilot

Notes. All flights apart from those marked are with J S R M-R at the controls all other are marked as D=Dual and 2nd = second pilot. This list only concerns types of aircraft so in some cases he did fly a number of different mark of these types.

1. De Havilland DH 82 Tiger Moth
2. Airspeed Oxford
3. Bristol Blenheim
4. Avro Anson
5. DH Leopard Moth
6. Hawker Audax
7. Lockheed Lodestar
8. Lockheed 12A
9. Lockheed Hudson
10. DH 89 Dominie
11. Percival Vega
12. Douglas DC3 D
13. DH Puss Moth
14. DH Hornet Moth
15. Curtis Hawk
16. Curtis Mohawk
17. B.A. Eagle (British Aircraft)
18. Bristol Beaufighter

19. N.A Harvard
20. Tipsy
21. Vultee Vengance
22. Hawker Typhoon
23. Vickers Wellington
24. Avro Lancaster
25. Percival Proctor
26. D.H. Mosquito
27. Fairey Barracuda
28. Vought Corsair
29. Supermarine Walrus
30. Handley Page Halifax
31. Bristol Brigand
32. Vickers Warwick
33. Consolidated Liberator D
34. Bristol Buckmaster
35. Supermarine Seafire
36. D.H. Vampire
37. Hawker Tempest
38. Avro Lincoln
39. Taylorcraft Auster
40. Gloster Meteor
41. Fairey Firefly
42. Olympia Glider known to be airworthy in 2012
43. Feisler Storch R.A.F. Museum Cosford
44. Percival Prentice
45. Zaun Konig*
46. Supermarine Spitfire
47. Vickers Viking
48. Sikorsky Hoverfly
49. Martin-Baker MB5
50. Ercoupe
51. Youngman-Bayne
52. Avro Tudor D

---

* This is how the name appears in the Farnborough log but it could also read as: 'Zaunkönig' (German for 'wren').

53.   D.H. Sea Hornet
54.   D.H. 108 Swallow
55.   Grumman Avenger
56.   Short Sturgeon
57.   Fairey Spearfish
58.   Hawker P1052
59.   Kranich, glider
60.   S28/43. (Blackburn Firecrest)
61.   Vickers Valetta

Stuart flew an impressive number of aircraft during his career. At least two of these were still in existence in 2020. There is also a glider that was used by the Empire Test Pilots' School that is still in existence and was still airworthy in 2012.

This is Feiseler Storch FI156-C-7, Work No 475081.

One of three Storch surrendered to the British at Flensburg, Germany in May 1945, this aircraft was coded RR+KE, previously coded GM+AK. This airframe was built in Czechoslovakia in 1944. The three aircraft were given the Air Ministry number of AM99, AM100 and AM101. The example flown by Stuart was AM101.This aircraft was delivered to the Royal Aircraft Establishment (RAE) at Farnborough on 5th September 1945. On 15th-17th September that year it was displayed at the Battle of Britain open days at Hendon. The aircraft was used extensively by the Aerodynamic Flight firstly to assess its characteristics and then as a tug for various types of glider. Being slow and extremely stable it made an ideal photography platform when studying the behaviour of rotor blades on the Sikorsky Hoverfly helicopter.

During November of '45 a German Aircraft Exhibition was held at Farnborough, this aircraft being one of the types flown. On 26th April 1946 AM101 was designated as one of eight German aircraft to remain in flying condition and given the RAF serial of VP546. The resident flying club at Farnborough used it extensively. In May 1946 Lt/ Cdr "Winkle" Brown carried out deck landing trails aboard HMS Triumph with VP546, the only German aircraft to land on a British carrier. During the summer of 1948, the aircraft was known to be at White Waltham, having been flown there by Stuart.

During 1949 and 1950 it resumed its previous role as a glider tug alongside that of camera platform for conducting smoke trail tests. In 1952 it was demonstrated at various venues, one of these being a slow flying demonstration at Wolverhampton followed by towing an Olympia glider for aerobatics. One of the other Storch had been used to keep it flying for as long as possible, but 1955 was to be the last year of use as, due to lack of spares, it was retired.

Initially allocated to RAF School Halton it was soon decided that it was not suitable for their needs so was then allocated to the Air Historical Branch. Located at several sites around the country VP546 had been extensively photographed for magazine articles, one of these in 1960 was for the Airfix Magazine when it returned to Luftwaffe colours. In 1969 it was considered for inclusion in the Battle of Britain Memorial Flight and restoration to airworthy condition was started but then abandoned due to a shortage of manpower and funds. Removed to RAF St Athan another attempt at restoring the aircraft began but again came to nothing. On the closure of St Athan VP546 eventually turned up at RAF Museum Cosford where it is still on display.

This article is based on text by Andrew Simpson, RAF Museum 2015.

Short Sturgeon, RK791. The development started during the Second World War with the requirement (S.6/430) for a high-performance reconnaissance/torpedo bomber for the Fleet Air Arm as a carrier borne aircraft. This was changed to S.11/43 which became the Sturgeon. Capable of carrying three cameras and armed with twin Browning .5inch machine guns in the nose, the aircraft could carry 1x1000lb bomb or 2x500lb bombs or 16x60lb Rocket Projectiles. The power plants were two Rolls Royce 140 engines. The first flight was on 7th June 1946. The end of the Second World War meant the cancellation of the order for these with only twenty-eight being built.

Hawker P1052, VX272. An experimental and developmental aircraft designed to evaluate the concept of swept wings to Air Ministry specification E38/46. This was an offshoot of N7/47 which became the Hawker Sea Hawk. VX272 was the first of two prototypes built at Hawker's Richmond factory. The aircraft was transported by road to Boscombe Down in November 1948 and first flown on 19th November by test pilot Trevor Wade. VX279, the second prototype first flew on 13th April 1949 and in May of that year Trevor Wade set a new record when he flew from London to Paris in 21 minutes and 28 seconds at an average speed of 618 miles per hour.

VX272 was delivered to Farnborough in June 1949 and Stuart Muller- Rowland took his first flight in it on 23rd June. The two prototypes took part in successful deck landing trials aboard HMS Eagle in May 1952. Powered by one 5000lb thrust RR Nene RN2 Turbojet. Span 31ft 6ins. Maximum Weight 13,488lb. Crew of 1. Maximum speed of 682mph at sea level, Mach 0.87 at 36,000ft. Service ceiling 45,500ft. VX 272 is in storage at the Fleet Air Arm Museum, Yeovilton.

Fairey Spearfish, RA360. The Spearfish was designed as a replacement for the Fairey Barracuda torpedo/dive bomber under Admiralty Specification O.5/43. Only five were built as was the case with several aircraft designed during the Second World War. The need for these being no longer required. The first prototype flew in July 1945 just before the cancellation of the contract. It was intended to carry internally, 4x 500lb bombs or 4 depth charges or a torpedo or finally an extra 180-gallon fuel tank could be fitted in the bomb bay. Additionally, 16x60lb rocket projectile could be carried on racks under the wings. Armament was to be 4x.5-inch Browning machine guns, two in a remotely controlled turret two in the wings. Power ix Bristol Centaurus 57 Radial 18-cylinder engine. Length 44ft 7ins. Wingspan 60ft 3ins. Maximum weight 22,083lbs. Maximum speed 292mph. Range 1036 miles. Service ceiling 25,000ft. Crew of 2.

S28/43 (unofficially known as the Blackburn Firecrest) VF172. To meet a requirement for a new carrier borne strike fighter for the Fleet Air Arm, design work on S28/43 began in October 1943 under the direction of Teddy Petter, chief designer at Blackburn. Work on the first prototype began in November. The Air Ministry issued specification S28/43 in February 1944. The programme became delayed very early on with proposals being put forward to build them with different engines: the original design using the Bristol Centaurus 77 driving a four bladed contra rotating propeller and the new proposal to use the Napier Sabre with the same propellers. A further delay came about with the late delivery of these propellers. The first prototype was not completed until February 1947, making its maiden flight on April 1st. By September of that year all three prototypes had been built and the third first flew in early 1948.

The aircraft had many faults, chiefly the position of the cockpit, being placed so far back the pilot had a very poor view for landing on carrier decks. The lengthy process of getting the prototypes built also meant that by the time they were ready they were almost obsolete, being overtaken by jet powered aircraft. Even before the first flight of the third prototype the Ministry of Supply had deemed it unsuitable for its intended purpose.

All three aircraft were used for testing the wing design with at least one (the third prototype VF172) going to RAE Farnborough. None of the airframes had many flying hours by 1950 when they returned to Blackburn at Brough to be scrapped.

Logbook of John Stuart Muller-Rowland 1st of August 1948-15th of February 1950

Month 1948	Date	Type	Aircraft No	Time T/O	Flight time	Passengers	Description of flight
August	13	Mosquito	RS641	1525	1hr	P L Bisgood	Distortion
"	16	Meteor	RA479	1505	35		High Altitude Research
"	17	Mosquito	RS641	1035	55		Distortion
"	18	Spitfire	NH403	906	15		Misc handling
"	18	Harvard	FT375	1215	30		Boundary layer
"	18	Spitfire	PM501	1450	1hr		Gust programme
"	18	Meteor	RA479	1635	40		High Altitude Research
"	19	Meteor	RA479	1435	40		High Altitude Research
"	20	Mosquito	RS641	1045	1hr	B R Townsend	Distortion
"	20	Mosquito	RS641	1455	1hr	Miss M Stedman	Distortion
"	23	Vampire	TG299	1115	45		Shock wave
"	23	Vampire	TG299	1515	45		Performance
"	24	Meteor	RA479	1005	45		High Altitude Research
"	24	Kranich	VP591	1715	1hr30		Ferry from Detling
"	25	Spitfire	NH403	855	15		Misc handling
"	25	Meteor	RA479	1505	50		High Altitude Research
"	26	Vampire	TG299	1030	30		Shock wave
"	27	Storch	VP456	1415	15		Towing VP591
"	27	Storch	VP456	1505	15		Towing VP591
"	27	Kranich	VP591	1535	30		Handling
"	27	Storch	VP456	1620	10		Towing VP591

	Date	Type	Serial	Time	Duration	Pilot	Purpose
"	30	Spitfire	PS914	1105	45		Gust programme
"	31	Spitfire	NH236	1510	1hr5 15hrs50		Prop research
Sept	1	Harvard	FT375	820	50	Mr W E Gray	Boundary layer
"	1	Harvard	FT375	1055	35	Mr W E Gray	Boundary layer
"	1	Harvard	FT375	1555	30	P W J Fullam	Boundary layer
"	2	Spitfire	NH403	920	15		Misc handling
"	3	Harvard	FT375	835	35	Mr W E Gray	Boundary layer
"	3	Harvard	FT375	1125	50	Mr W E Gray	Boundary layer
"	3	Vampire	TG299	1030	40		Performance
"	3	Vampire	TG299	1510	45		Performance
"	6	Meteor	RA479	1050	50		High Altitude Research
"	6	Spitfire	RS941	1505	45		Gust programme
"	6	Meteor	RA479	1630	45		High Altitude Research
"	8	Vampire	TG299	955	30		Performance
"	9	Spitfire	PM501	930	40		Gust programme
"	10	Harvard	FT375	905	25	Mr P W J Fullam	Boundary layer
"	10	Kranich	VP591	1110	1hr	Pilot F/Lt Ellis, pass	Ferry to Detling
"	10	Storch	VP546	1500	1hr	J M-R	Ferry from Detling
"	17	Storch	VP546	1040	50	F/Lt Ellis	Ferry to Detling
"	17	Storch	VP546	1335	1hr20	Pilot F/Lt Ellis, pass	Towing VP591 from Detling
"	17	Storch	VP546	1625	30	J M-R	Ferry to Boscombe Down

Date	Aircraft	Serial	Time	Duration	Crew/Notes	Remarks
" 17	Vampire	VF343	1730	15		Ferry from Boscombe Down
" 21	Spitfire	PS914	1015	42		Gust programme
" 21	Storch	VP546	1125	15		Ferry to Odiham
" 22	Spitfire	PM501	1030	5		Gust programme
" 24	Spitfire	PS914	1050	30		Gust programme
" 24	Spitfire	NH403	1445	30		Misc handling
" 28	Mosquito	RS641	1435	45	Pass P L Bisgood	Distortion
" 29	Spitfire	PS914	1010	50		Gust programme
" 29	Lancaster	DS708	1605	1hr	Pass J M Lawrence, J G Walker	Servo tab Control
" 30	Mosquito	RS641	1610	50	K N Smith, plus 1 / Pass P L Bisgood	Distortion
				20hrs55		
Oct 4	Spitfire	PS914	1100	1hr15		Gust Programme
" 4	Mosquito	RS657	1630	25		Test flight
" 4	Mosquito	RS657	1955	50		Night flying practice
" 5	Mosquito	RS657	1055	50	Lt Cdr Brown, Flying DH108 / Lt Cdr Brown.	Ferry to Hatfield
" 5	Mosquito	RS657	1505	20	Hatfield	Ferry from Hatfield
" 6	Hurricane	L3687	1205	40		Boundary layer
" 6	Spitfire	PS914	1545	40		Gust programme
" 7	Harvard	FT375	1015	25		Boundary layer
" 7	Harvard	FT375	1110	10		Boundary layer

	Day	Type	Serial	Time	Duration	Pilot	Purpose
"	7	Meteor	RA479	1145	50		High Altitude Research
"	7	Hurricane	L3687	1550	25		Boundary layer
"	8	Prentice	VN684	1455	1hr	Pilot Lt Cdr Brown, pass J M-R	Misc handling
"	12	Spitfire	PS914	1100	1hr10		Gust programme
"	13	Mosquito	RS641	1425	45	P L Bisgood	Distortion
"	15	Hurricane	L3687	1640	20		Boundary layer
"	18	Spitfire	PS914	1420	40		Gust programme
"	19	Meteor	RA479	1225	45		High Altitude Research
"	19	Spitfire	PM501	1530	35		Gust programme
"	19	Meteor	RA479	1655	50		High Altitude Research
"	20	Mosquito	RS641	1020	50	P L Bisgood	Distortion
"	20	Harvard	FT375	1250	15		Ferry to Boscombe Down
"	20	Harvard	FT375	1550	25		Ferry from Boscombe Down
"	21	Storch	VX154	1010	15	S/L Ellis	Test flight
"	21	Hurricane	L3687	1145	40		Boundary layer
"	21	Meteor	RA479	1505	45		High Altitude Research
"	22	Spitfire	PS914	1030	45		Gust programme
"	25	Mosquito	RS641	1450	5	P L Bisgood	Distortion
"	26	Mosquito	RS641	1125	50	P L Bisgood	Distortion
"	28	Meteor	RA479	1150	50		High Altitude Research
"	29	Hurricane	L3687	1025	45		Boundary layer
"	29	Harvard	FT375	1530	55	R C A Dando	Boundary layer
					20hrs 20		

		Aircraft	Reg	Time	Dur	Crew/Pass	Remarks
Nov	3	Youngman Baines	VT789		15		Test flight
"	4	Anson	NL200	850	20	Pass, S W Chisman, G S Collis	Ferry to Lee on Solent
"	4	Anson	NL200	950	30		Ferry from Lee on Solent
"	4	Spitfire	PS914	1045	45		Gust programme
"	4	Mosquito	RS641	1155	25	Pass L Batcelor	Test flight
"	4	Hurricane	L3687	1520	20		Boundary layer
"	4	Lancaster	DS708	1615	30	Pass, S/L Lawrence, K W Smith, R D Dennis, A R Bramwell	Servo tab Control
"	5	Harvard	FT375	1040	50		Ferry to Desford
"	5	Harvard	FT375	1645	45		Ferry from Desford
"	8	Hurricane	L3687	1600	25		Boundary layer
"	9	Youngman Baines	VT789	1035	45		High lift
"	10	Youngman Baines	VT789	955	45		High lift
"	10	Meteor	RA479	1115	40		High Altitude Research
"	11	Hurricane	L3687	1040	20		Boundary layer
"	11	Harvard	FT375	1410	30	Pilot, S/L Ellis, pass, J M-R	Ferry to Hatfield
"	11	Vampire	VV137	1520	20		Ferry from Hatfield

Date	Aircraft	Serial	Time	Duration	Pass, instructor, S/L	Remarks
" 15	Oxford	LX308	1100	1hr15	Genders	Instructor pilot rating
" 15	Meteor	VT259	1550	40		Fuel boiling
" 16	Storch	VP546	1105	5	Pilot, S/L Genders, pass	Return to base, radio U/S
" 16	Storch	VP546	1145	30	S/L Robinson, J M-R	Ferry to Andover
" 16	Storch	VP546	1415	40	Pilot, S/L Genders, pass J M-R	Ferry from Andover
" 17	Mosquito	RS641	955	45	P L Bisgood	Distortion
" 17	Mosquito	RS641	1425	50	Miss M Stedman	Distortion
" 17	Vampire	TG299	1555	20		Test flight
" 18	Valetta	VL268	1005	1hr	Pilot, S/L Havercroft, Drake	
" 18	Valetta	VL268	1525	35	S L Brown, J M-R	Handling
" 19	Mosquito	RS641	1455	55	Drake	Handling
" 23	Mosquito	RS641	1415	55	P L Bisgood	Distortion
" 24	Mosquito	RS641	1105	5	P L Bisgood	Distortion
" 24	Vampire	TG299	1215	15	S/L Lawrence	Test flight
" 25	Vampire	TG299	1420	20		Boundary layer
" 25	Vampire	TG299	1535	20		Boundary layer
" 26	Vampire	TG299	1215	20		Boundary layer
				18hrs50		
Dec 1	Vampire	TG299	1145	45		Boundary layer

					Crew/Passengers	Remarks
" 1	Spitfire	PS914	1445	15		Test flight
" 2	Vampire	TG299	1010	15		Boundary layer
" 3	Spitfire	PS914	1125	20		Gust programme
" 6	Lancaster	DS708	1155	55	Pass, S/L Lawrence, J S Walker, A R Mottram, Miss M Stedman	Servo tab Control
" 7	Vampire	TG299	1520	45		Performance
" 8	Spitfire	PS914	1100	1hr30		Gust programme
" 10	Vampire	TG299	1030	50		Performance
" 14	Spitfire	PM501	1420	1hr50		Gust programme
" 15	Vampire	TG299	1055	45		Performance
" 15	Vampire	TG299	1440	50		Shock wave
" 15	Lancaster	DS708	1545	35	Pass, S/L Lawrence, J S Walker, B R Townsend, Miss M Stedman	
" 15	Buckmaster	RP243	1805	25	Pass, W C Chamberlain	Instructor Presentation
" 20	Lancaster	DS708	1515	1hr	Pass, S/L Lawrence, J S Walker	Servo tab Control
" 21	Meteor	RA479	1405	5	B R Townsend	Test flight
" 21	Lancaster	DS708	1525	1hr5	S/L Lawrence, J S Walker	Servo tab Control

1949		Aircraft	Serial	Time	12hrs5	B R Townsend, Miss M Stedman	Servo tab Control
Jan	6	Meteor	VW417	1055	35	Pass, F/Lt Morrison	Speed and mach number
"	6	Meteor	RA479	1530	45		High Altitude Research
"	10	Vampire	TG299	1040	50		Performance
"	10	Vampire	VL530	1625	15		Performance
"	11	Meteor	RA479	1045	1hr		High Altitude Research
"	11	Meteor	VL530	1230	30		Fuel boiling
"	11	Meteor	RA479	1510	55		High Altitude Research
"	12	Meteor	RA479	1100	40		High Altitude Research
"	13	Vampire	TG299	1030	45		Performance
"	13	Lancaster	DS708	1205	35	Pass, S/L Lawrence, J S Walker	Servo tab Control
"	13	Lancaster	DS708	1520	40	Pass, S/L Lawrence, S/L Hazeldene	Handling
"	14	Lancaster	DS708	1055	45	Pass, S/L Brook, K W Smith	Handling
"	17	Spitfire	PM501	1215	1hr	S/L Lawrence	Gust programme
"	17	Lancaster	DS708	1055	40	Pass, S/L Lawrence, Bryce,	Servo tab Control
"	18	Meteor	RA479	1050	40	J S Walker, Somers	High Altitude Research

Date	Type	Reg.	Time	Duration	Remarks	Purpose
" 19	Meteor	RA479	1120	50		High Altitude Research
" 20	Spitfire	PS914	1215	50		Test flight
" 20	Harvard	FT375	1455	30		Ferry to Boscombe Down
" 25	Meteor	RA479	955	45		High altitude research
" 26	Storch	VP546	1015	15		Test flight
" 27	Meteor	RA479	1355	50		High Altitude Research
" 27	Meteor	RA479	1534	50		High Altitude Research
" 28	Vampire	TG299	1150	1hr		Performance
" 28	Vampire	TG328	1525	30		Performance
" 31	Meteor	RA479	1150	45		High Altitude Research
" 31	Meteor	RA479	1530	35		High Altitude Research
				18hrs 10		
Feb 1	Meteor	RA479	1220	40	Pilot, S/L Smith, pass, J M-R	High altitude research
" 1	Storch	VP546	1500	30	F/Lt Morrison	
" 1	Vampire	VT793	1600	15		Ferry to Lee on Solent
" 2	Meteor	RA479	1120	40		Ferry from Lee on Solent
" 2	Ercoupe	VX147	1600	30	Pass, A R Cawthorne	High altitude research
" 3	Meteor	RA479	1110	45		Performance
" 4	Vampire	VF343	1205	40		High altitude research
" 7	Meteor	RA479	1215	55		Wing flow
" 8	Meteor	RA479	1055	35		High altitude research
" 8	Meteor	RA479	1500	40		High altitude research

Month	Day	Type	Serial	Time	Mins	Crew / Notes	Purpose
"	9	Vampire	TG299	1030	50		Performance
"	9	Vampire	TG299	1500	50		Performance
"	11	Vampire	TG299	1110	40		Performance
"	11	S28/43	VF172	1625	30	3rd prototype.	Power controls
"	14	Ercoupe	VX147	1555	35	Pass, S/L Lawrence	Performance
"	15	Lancaster	PP755	1155	35	Pass, S/L Lawrence, S/L Smith	
"	15	Ercoupe	VX147	1555	35	R J Ross, B R Townsend	Power controls
"	16	Vampire	TG299	1210	55	Pass, R J Ross	Performance
"	17	Storch	VP546	1350	35	Pilot, S/L Smith, pass, J M-R	Performance
"	17	Vampire	TG328	1555	15		Ferry from Lee on Solent
"	18	Spitfire	PM501	1050	25		Flex deck at Lee on Solent
		DH108				J M-R, first flight in DH108	Gust programme
"	22	Swallow	TG238	1650	25		Handling
"	22	Vampire	TG299	1155	45		Performance
"	23	Vampire	TG299	1120	50		Performance
"	28	Vampire	TG299	1150	45		Performance
					33hrs30		
Mar	2	Spitfire	NH403	1610	25		Misc Handling
"	3	Vampire	TG299	1140	40		Performance
"	4	Lancaster	PP755	1100	30	Pass, S/L Lawrence, S/L Smith	

Date	Type	Serial	Time	Duration	Passengers/Crew	Notes
6	Vampire	TG299	1040	40	B R Townsend	Power controls
8	Lancaster	PP755	1020	1hr10	Pass, S/L Lawrence, P M Davey	Performance
9	S28/43	VF172	1030	55	B R Townsend	Power controls
9	Harvard	FT375	1340	1hr10	Pass, J M-R	Ferry to Brough
10	Storch	VP546	1025	10		Ferry from Brough
10	Storch	VP546	1100	5	Pass, Lt/Cdr Brown	Ferry to Blackbushe
10	Vampire	TG299	1130	50		Ferry from Blackbushe
14	Lancaster	PP755	1025	55	Pass, S/L Lawrence, H W Smith	Performance
15	Meteor	RA479	1100	55	P M Davey, G H Elsley	Power controls / High altitude research
16	Lancaster	PP755	1450	1hr	Pass, S/L Lawrence, H W Smith	Power controls
17	Harvard	FT375	1015	25	P M Davey, G H Elsley	Ferry to Boscombe Down
17	Harvard	FT375	1630	25	Pass, D J Lyons	Ferry from Boscombe Down
17	Prentice	VR307		45	Pass, D J Lyons	Spinning at Boscombe Down
17	Prentice	TV172		1hr5		Spinning at Boscombe Down
21	Mosquito	RS641	1655	10		Ferry to Lasham

	Date	Type	Serial	Time	Duration	Pilot/Passenger	Purpose
"	21	Storch	VP546	1725	15	Pilot, F/Lt Smith, pass, J M-R	Ferry from Lasham
"	22	Spitfire	PM501	1145	35		Gust programme
"	22	Storch	VP546	1415	25	Pass, Lt Elliot	Ferry to Lee on Solent
"	22	Storch	VP546	1535	35		Ferry from Lee on Solet
"	22	DH108	TG283	1620	35		Approach and landing
"	23	Meteor	RA479	1100	45		High altitude research
"	24	Meteor	RA479	1600	45		High altitude research
"	25	Spitfire	PM501	1420	30		Gust programme
"	28	Meteor	RA479	1510	40		High altitude research
"	29	Spitfire	PM501	1200	35		Gust programme
					17hrs50		
April	1	Meteor	RA479	1020	40		High altitude research
"	1	Meteor	RA479	1500	40		High altitude research
"	1	Harvard	FT375	1630	25		Ferry to Hatfield
"	1	Harvard	FT375	1720	25	Pass, Lt Elliot	Ferry from Hatfield
"	4	Meteor	RA479	1125	45		High Altitude Research
"	5	Spitfire	PM501	1015	25		Gust programme
"	6	Meteor	RA479	1430	50		High Altitude Research
"	7	Meteor	RA479	1240	10		High Altitude Research
"	7	Vampire	TG299	1555	50		Performance
"	8	Harvard	FT375	1155	20		Ferry to Chilbolton
"	8	Harvard	FT375	1250	20	Pass, Lt Mancus	Ferry from Chilbolton
"	8	Meteor	VW412	1600	40	Pass, W J Charmley	Speed and mach number

Date	Aircraft	Serial	Time	Min	Passenger / Notes	Purpose
" 11	Lancaster	DS708	1615	40	Pass, F/Lt Beddow, J S Walker	Servo tab Control
" 13	Vampire	TG299	1505	35	B R Townsend	Performance
" 14	Spitfire	PM501	1015	30		Gust programme
" 19	Meteor	RA479	1405	30		High Altitude Research
" 20	Spitfire	PM501	1040	40		Misc Handling
" 21	Vampire	TG299	1605	10		Performance
" 22	Vampire	VF343	1000	35	Forced landed at Boscome Down	Wing flow
" 27	Vampire	TG299	1400	50		Performance
" 27	Vampire	TG299	1545	10		From Boscombe Down
" 28	Meteor	RA479	1450	35		High Altitude Research
" 29	Vampire	TG299	1600	45		Performance
				12hrs35		
1949 May 2	Devon	VP959	1605	40	S/Ldr Hithchen	Dual Control
" 3	Spitfire	NH403	1550	30		Misc handling
" 4	Vampire	VF343	1445	40	H W Smith, H Lawrence	Wing flow
" 5	Lancaster	PP775	1115	35		Powered controls
" 5	Vampire	TG299	1100	45		Performance
" 6	Vampire	VT802	1555	15		To Lee on Solent
" 10	Vampire	VF343	1610	30		Wind flow

Date	Aircraft	Serial	Time	Duration	Pilot	Notes
" 11	Harvard	FT375	850	15		Boundary layer
" 12	Vampire	TG299	1045	45		Performance
" 16	Spitfire	PM501	1505	55		Gust programme / Force Landed
"	"	"	1650	20		Cranfield
" 17	Vampire	VF343	1520	35		Wing flow
" 18	Meteor	EE476	1450	55		Snaking
" 19	Vampire	VG701	1500	35		Flex deck from Tangmere
" 20	Vampire	VG701	1545	20		Flex deck from Tangmere
" 23	Vampire	VG701	1510	15	F/L Adshead P M Davey	Flex deck from Lee on Solent
" 25	Lancaster	PP775	1110	25		Powered controls
" 25	DH108 Youngman Baynes	VW120	1510	30		Approach and Landing
" 26	Meteor	VT789	1500	35	W G M Poat	High lift
" 27	Harvard	FT375	1020	20	"	Misc handling
"	"	"	1120	20		" "
" 30	Meteor	RA479	1615	30		High Altitude research
				11hr15		
June 1	Meteor	RA479	1515	25	J E Morrell	High Altitude research
" 2	Harvard	FT375	1015	10	H W Smith, H Lawrence	Misc handling
"	Harvard	FT375	1155	10	H T Slater	Misc handling
"	Lancaster	PP775	1455	55	H W Smith F/O Capper	Powered controls

Day	Aircraft	Reg	Time	Duration	Crew	Remarks
9	Youngman Baynes	VT789	1155	35		High lift
"	Lancaster	PP775	1605	40		Powered controls
10	Oxford	MP449	1550	50		Instructor pilot rating
12	Meteor	RA479	1300	40		High Altitude research
14	Harvard	FT375	1035	40		Ferry to Wellesbourne
"	Meteor	RA479	1420	35		High Altitude research
15	Oxford	MP449	1150	1hr 15	Puttick	Instructor pilot rating
	Youngman Baynes	VT789	1500	55		High lift
16	Meteor	RA479	1610	40		High Altitude research
17	Meteor	RA479	950	40		High Altitude research
20	Seafire	SX252	1140	35		Ferry to Bramcote
21	Spitfire	NH403	1210	5		Test
22	Youngman Baynes	VT789	1045	50	D R H Puttick	High lift
	Meteor	RA479	1520	30		High Altitude research
23	Youngman Baynes	VT789	915	1hr		High lift
	P1052	VX272	1200	30	Lawrence, Townsend, Thornton	Flight tests
24	Harvard	FT375	925	10		Weather test
	Harvard	FT375	1000	1hr 5		Ferry to and from Wellesbourne
28	Lancaster	DS708	1435	45		Servo Tabs

Date	No.	Aircraft	Serial	Time	Duration	Crew	Remarks
"	29	Spitfire	PM501	1635	35		Ferry to and from Hatfield
"	30	Vampire	VW412	1620	25		High Mach no
					14hr45		
July	1	DH108	TG283	1110	30	F/L Adshead, H W Smith, G Roberts	Approach and Landing
"	4	Lancaster	PP775	1635	35	G/Capt John Cunningham pilot	Powered controls
"	5	Lancaster	PP775	1520	35	G R Townsend, A R Mottam Thornton	Powered controls
"	6	Lancaster	PP775	1150		G R Townsend, A R Mottam	Powered controls
"		DH108	VW120	1515	40		High speed stability
"	7	DH108	VW120	1115	45		High speed stability
"		Lancaster	DS708	1540	1hr		Servo Tabs
"	8	Lancaster	PP775	1145	40		Powered controls
"			VP587	1735	1hr		Ferry to Detling
"	9		VP587	1045	1hr		Ferry to Detling
"	10	Youngman Baynes	VT789	1045	1hr		High lift
"		DH108	TG283	1450	30		Approach and Landing
"	12	Youngman Baynes	VT789	1515	30		High lift
"	13	Youngman Baynes	VT789	1030	40		High lift

Date	Aircraft	Reg	Time	Duration	Passenger	Speed and Mach No
	Meteor	VW412	1630	20		Speed and Mach No
15	Youngman Baynes	VT789	1810	5		From Blackbushe
"	P1052	VX272	1705	1hr25		Flight tests
18	Youngman Baynes	VT789	1110	5		High lift
19	P1052	VX272	1505	1hr25		Test Flight
20	Vampire	TG299	1100	20		Test flight
21	Vampire	TG299	1545	25		Shock wave
"	Vampire	TG 299	1055	15		Demonstration
22	DH108	VW120	1055	25		High Speed stability
27	Oxford	MP449	1025	1hr10		Instructor pilot rating
"	Spitfire	PM501	1500	45		Gust programme/ Force Landed
26	Youngman Baynes	VT789	950	45		High lift
"	Lancaster	DS708	1605	35		Servo Tabs
27	Vampire	TG299	1050	50		Shock wave
"	Spitfire	PM501	1445	25		test flight
				18hr55		
August 2	Vampire	TG299	1050	50	Miss E Podger, Miss	Shock wave
3	Lancaster	DS708	1555	40	P N Richards	Servo Tabs
5	Dominie	NR728	925	50	G R Goffe	Ferry to Westcott and return
"	Youngman Baynes	VT789	1105	50		High lift

	No	Type	Serial	Time	Duration	Notes
		Harvard	FT375	1420	40	Test Flight
"	11	Vampire	TG299	1525	50	Shock wave
"	12	Meteor	VW412	1535	50	Speed and Mach No
"	15	Lancaster	DS708	1105	1hr	Servo Tabs
		Lancaster	DS708	1625	15	Servo Tabs
"	16	Harvard	FT375	1035	1hr25	Ferry to Odiham
		Lancaster	PP775	1630	35	Powered controls
"	17	Lancaster		1530	45	
"	18	P1052	VX272	1600	45	Test E38/46
„	19	Vampire	TG299	1210	45	High Mach no
"	22	Vampire	TG299	1635	50	High Mach no
"	23	P1052	VX272	1145	10	Test 38/46
"	24	P1052	VX272	1635	1hr	Test 38/46
"	25	Avenger	KE436		25	Catapulting 5mins each launch
"		Meteor	EE476	1615	30	Snaking
"	26	Spearfish	RA360	1125	5	Test flight
		Mosquito	HI898	1415	30	Handling
"	29	Lancaster	DS708	1101	20	Servo tabs
		P1052	VX272	1215	1hr20	Test E38/46
"	30	Avenger	KE436	1110	1hr25	Ferry from Sydenham
		Sturgeon	RK791	1615	1hr15	Ferry from Sydenham
					18hr50	

It appears that JSM-R did not fly between 12/9/49 and 18/11/49

211

Sept	1	Lancaster	DS708	1050	15		Servo tabs
"	2	Lancaster	DS708	1445	35		Servo tabs
"	2	Meteor	EE594	1420	20		Instructional Presentation
"	5	Avenger	KE436	1125	75		To Wolverhampton and return
"	8	P1052	VX272	915	1hr		Test E38/46
"	12	P1052	VX272	825	55		Test E38/46
					4hr30		
Nov	18	DH108	VW120	1425	35		Handling
"	21	Lancaster	DS708	1205	1hr20		Servo tabs
"	22	DH108	TG283	1155	35		High speed stability
"	24	Harvard	FT375	1010	50		To Wolverhampton
"	28	Avenger	KE446	1600	5		Catapulting
"	29	Lancaster	DS708	1350	1hr15		Servo tabs
"	30	DH108	VW120	1045	35	Passenger	High speed stability, Odiham
					5hr 15		
Dec	2	Lancaster	DS708				Servo Tabs
"	7	Vampire	TG299	1055	25		Shock wave
"	8	Storch	VP546	1000	10		To Odiham
		DH108	VW120	1340	40		High speed stability, Odiham
		DH108	VW120		40		Return
"	9	Storch	VX154		10		To Odiham
		DH108	VW120	1155	30		High speed stability, Odiham
		DH108	VW120	1325	30		Return
"	12	Storch	VP546	1045	40		To Brooklands and return

	Date	Aircraft	Reg	Time	Duration	Crew	Remarks
"	13	DH108	VW120	1220	40		High speed stability
"	14	DH108	VW120	1428	40		High speed stability
"	15	DH108	VW120	1005	40		High speed stability
"	16	Storch	VP546	1410	20		Ferry to Odiham and return
"	19	Lancaster	DS708	1155	1hr	K Elliott	Servo Tabs
"	20	Storch	VP546	1435	40		Ferry to Chilbolton and return
"		Harvard	FT375	845	40		Ferry to Chilbolton and return
"	22	Brigand	RH748	1055	30		Ferry to Hatfield
"		Brigand	RH748	1550	30		Return
					9hr 20		
1950							
Jan	10	Vampire	VT804	1045	20		Flex deck
"	11	DH108	TG283	1425	1hr		Approach and Landing
"	12	Lancaster	PP775	1100	1hr	Beddow, Smith, Kerr, Townsend	Powered controls
"	13	Storch	VP546	1510	1hr		Ferry to Gosport
"		Storch	VP546	940	20		Return
"	18	Vampire	VT804	1305	50		Flex deck
"		Harvard	FT375	1645	50		To Wolverhampton
"		Harvard	FT375	940	20		Return
"	19	Vampire	VT804	1145	25		Flex deck
"	20	Vampire	VF343	1135	25		Wing flow
"	23	Storch	VP546	1620	25		To White Waltham
"		Storch	VP546				Return

		Type	Serial			Remarks
"	24	DH108	TG283	1100	25	Approach and Landing
"					7hr 20	
Feb	2	Avenger	KE436	1010	55	Ferry to Wolverhampton
"	3	Vampire	VV215	1125	40	Snaking
"	6	Lancaster	RE131	1430	20	Power elevator control
"	7	Spitfire	PM501	915	1hr	Ferry to Woodbridge
"	8	Vampire	VT795	1140	15	Flex deck
"	10	Vampire	VV215	1115	35	Snaking
"	14	DH108	VW120	1540	30	High speed test
"	15	DH108	VW120	1115	15	High speed test. Crashed near Bletchley. J S R Muller- Rowland Killed, his body found nearby.
					4hr30	
					264hrs 15	Total for Aug 1948-Feb 1950
					2380hrs55	Total for service career
						Total for DH108 10hrs55mins

214

Empire Test Pilots School Detailed Course Syllabus

Taken from the ETPS handbook for 1951 course No 11. This syllabus does not differ much from course No. 6 that Stuart took in 1947. Although some advances had been made between the two courses, this gives a good indication of what he would have done. Some of the instructors mentioned may well have been different. Stuart's logbook for the period he attended ETPS corresponds with much of the flying programme.

Flying syllabus in italics.

Week I.
First Day, Tuesday.
0900. Completion of arrival forms.
1000. Introductory talk by the Commandant.
1015. Talk by the Chief Test Flying Instructor (CTFI).
1045. Talk by the Chief Technical Instructor.
1120. Talk on Traffic Control Facilities by the Senior Traffic Controller, RAE.
1230-1345. Lunch.
1345. Issue of Flying Clothing etc.
Wednesday, Thursday, Friday. Lecture programme.
1845. *Mathematics and applied Mechanics (revision). Report writing, by Chief Technical Instructor (CTI). *Note: Additional tutorial classes (optional) will be arranged each morning at 1100 and each afternoon at 1430.

Familiarisation flying on School aircraft.
During the period students should make themselves familiar with the School orders and local flying restrictions. They should also study local maps and pilots' notes relating to School aircraft.

Week 2.
Properties of gases and the standard atmosphere. Elements of aircraft and engine performance. Elementary aerodynamics, by CTI.
Preliminary handling testing: – Cockpit assessment, ground handling, take-off and landing, by CFTI.
Familiarisation flying on School aircraft- this will be an extension of the programme for the previous week but will include some preliminary handling exercises and exercises in observation and report writing.

Week 3.
Speed measurements. The performance equation, by CTI.
Preliminary Handling tests: – spins and stalls.
Performance testing: – Preliminary climbs, by CFI.
As previous week but extending to include elementary performance exercises, practice climbs and the determination of full throttle heights.
During the week, evening lecture at Royal Aeronautical Society.

Week 4.
Performance reduction methods, by CTI.
Preliminary handling tests: – aerobatics & handling at high speeds, by CTFI.
Note: a progress test will be made during this week.
As previous week.

Week 5.
Routine reduction of climb and level speed results. System of take-off measurement, by ATI.

Performance tests: – Partial climbs, by CTFI.

The handling of jet engines, by lecturer from Rolls Royce.

Consolidation of preliminary handling tests and exercises. Partial climb measurements and reductions and preparation for ceiling climb and level speed measurements.

Visit to the Science Museum and Royal Aeronautical Society.

Week 6.

Speed measurement and compressibility effects. Position error, by CTI.

Performance testing; – ceiling climbs and levels. Position error measurement. Determination of climb max, by CTFI.

Visual aids, by Mr E.S. Calvert, RAE.

Ceiling climbs and level speed determination. Climbs will be carried out using the partial climb results previously determined as a basis for the recommended climbing speed. Handling. Continuation of preliminary handling exercises and report writing.

Week 7.

Jet propulsion- the performance equation and dimensional analysis, by CTI. Jet aircraft performance testing: – climbs and levels, by CTFI.

Physiological aspects of test flying, by W/C Ruffel-Smith, Institute of Aviation Medicine.

Aims and objectives of research at RAE, by Mr W.G.A Perring, RAE.

Performance and handling tests. As during previous week but extended to include position error measurements.

Royal Aeronautical Society Lecture.

Week 8.

Cooling tests. Jet propulsion reduction methods. Introduction of fuel consumption and range flying, by CTI.

Flight test development of reciprocating engines, by Mr

H.T. Edgecombe, Bristol Aircraft.

Note, a performance test will be made this week.

Continuation of handling tests. Climbs and levels on jet propelled aircraft.

Groups A and B will visit the Institute of Aviation Medicine.

Week 9.

Fuel consumption and range testing. Weighing and centre of gravity of aircraft, by CTI.

Cooling tests, by CTFI.

Engineering and functional tests, by Lecturer from A.A.E.E.

A previous week, extended to begin fuel consumption measurements. Continuation of handling tests.

Groups C and D will visit the Institute of Aviation Medicine.

Week 10.

First tour of the aviation industry. (*Author's note: as seen in the chapter on Stuart*).

Week 11.

Fuel consumption and range tests. Introduction to longitudinal stability, by CTI.

Range and fuel consumption testing, by CTFI.

Aircraft instrumentation, by Lecturer from RAE

General performance and handling tests.

Groups A and B will visit RAE Instrumentation Division.

Week 12.

Longitudinal stability, by CTI.

Qualitative handling, by CTFI.

Air photography, by Lecturer from RAE.

Instrumentation, by Lecturer from RAE.

Continuation of performance measurements and extension of general handling exercises.

Groups C and D will visit RAE Instrumentation Division.

Week 13.

Routine reduction of fuel consumption results. Longitudinal stability (continued), by CTI.

Preliminary longitudinal stability and handling, by CTFI.

Automatic controls, by Lecturer from RAE.

Continuation of performance measurements and handling exercises.

Groups A and B will visit Instrument and Photography Division, RAE.

Week 14.

Fuel consumption measurements- Jet propelled aircraft, by CTFI.

Strength of aircraft, by Lecturer from RAE.

Propeller gas turbines, by Mr A.C. Clinton, Bristol

Note, a progress test will be made during this week.

Fuel consumption measurements. Longitudinal stability measurements. General handling exercises.

Groups C and D will visit Instrument and Photography Division, RAE.

All day visit to aircraft firm.

Week 15.

Qualitative handling at high altitudes and speed, by CTFI.

Supply dropping, by Lecturer from RAE.

Flight testing at high speeds, by Mr John Derry, De Havilland.

Flutter, by Lecturer from RAE.

Fuel consumption measurements and longitudinal stability measurements. General handling exercises.

Group A and B will visit RAE Structures and Mechanical Engineering Divisions.

Week 16.
Pressure cabins, by Lecturer from RAE.
Gliding, by Mr Lorne Welch
Mid-course examinations.
As previous week.
Groups C and D will visit RAE Structures and Mechanical
Engineering Divisions.

Week 17.
Measurements of side slip, by Mr W.B. Gerard, armament
division, RAE.
As previous week.

Weeks 18 & 19.

Two weeks mid-course leave.

Week 20.
Longitudinal stability and manoeuvrability, by CTI.
Longitudinal stability and manoeuvrability measure-
ments, by CTFI.
*Continuation of handling tests, extension to include more
advanced exercises in stability and manoeuvrability
assessments and measurements.*
Groups A and B will visit RAE Accident Investigation
Department.

Week 21.
Lateral and directional stability, by CTI.
Stability and manoeuvrability measurements, by CFTI.
As previous week.
Groups C and D will visit RAE Accident Investigation
Department.

Week 22.
Asymmetric handling tests, CTFI.
Aircraft performance measurements, (Recent
Developments), by Lecturer from A.A.E.E.

As previous week.
Groups A and B will visit Radio and Radar Department, RAE.
Visits to industrial firms.

Week 23.
Asymmetric handling tests, by CTFI.
Control and behaviour assessment, (Recent Developments), by Lecturer from A.A.E.E.
Note, Progress tests will be made during this week.
As previous week extended to include asymmetric handling tests.
Groups C and D will visit Radio and Radar Department, RAE.

Week 24.
Comprehensive handling. Asymmetric handling tests (continued).
Consolidation of performance handling, control stability and manoeuvrability tests.
Students or groups will be allocated aircraft to prepare comprehensive handling tests.

Week 25.
Comprehensive handling (continued), by CTFI.
The work of Naval Aircraft Department, by Lecturer from RAE.
Carrier landing and take-off aids, by Lecturer from RAE.
As previous week.
Groups A and B will visit Naval Aircraft Division.
Visit to industrial firm.

Week 26.
Determination of centre of gravity limits, by CTFI.
Test requirements for civil aircraft, by Lecturer from RAE.
Civil aircraft requirements, by Lecturers from BEA or BOAC.

As previous week. Lateral and directional stability; changes of trim with speed and power variation; determination of centre of gravitity.
Groups C and D will visit Naval Aircraft Division.
Visit to industrial firm.

Week 27.
Bombing equipment, by Lecturer from RAE.
Aircraft testing from the Armament Department, by Lecturer from A.A.E.E.
Rocket weapon development, by Lecturer from RAE.
As previous week.
Groups A and B will visit Armament Department, RAE.

Week 28.
The RAE wind tunnels, by Lecturer from RAE.
The work of A.A.E.E., by Chief Superintendent, A.A.E.E.
Groups C and D will visit Armament Department.
Visit to A.A.E.E., Boscombe Down and an industrial firm.

Week 29.
Special lectures will be arranged during SBAC week.
Visit to RAE wind tunnels.
SBAC Show. (*Author's note: Farnborough*).

Week 30.

Tour of aircraft industry or overseas establishments to be arranged.

Week 31.
The work of Aero Flight, by Head of Aero Flight, RAE.
(*Author's note: Position that Stuart held later*).
Aircraft control problems.
Rotary wing aircraft (*Author's note: helicopters*), by Lecturers from Aero Flight, RAE.
Continuation of stability and handling.
Groups A and B will visit Aero Flight, RAE.

Week 32.

High speed flight problems. Take-off and landing problems.

Helicopter flight testing, Lecturers from Aero Flight, RAE.

High speed aircraft design, by Mr P. Wreford-Bushe, Hawker.

Continuation of stability and handling tests.

Groups C and D will visit Aero Flight, RAE.

Week 33.

Rockets as power plants, by Dr Merrington, RPD.

The work of supersonics division, by head of S.D., RAE.

Aerodynamics of supersonic aircraft, by Lecturer from S.D., RAE.

Tailless aircraft, by Lecturer from RAE.

As previous week.

Groups A and B will visit Supersonics Division.

Week 34.

Rocket propulsion, by Mr A.V. Cleaver, de Havilland.

Investigation of supersonic airflow, by Lecturer from S.D., RAE.

Freely flying models in the transonic range, by Lecturer from S.D., RAE.

As previous week.

Groups C and D will visit Supersonics Division, RAE.

Week 35.

Tour of the aircraft industry.

Week 36.

The work of M.A.E.E., by Lecturer from M.A.E.E., Felixstowe.

Airborne supply, by Lecturer from A.A.E.E.

Operational requirements of Coastal Command, by Lecturer from Coastal Command.

Revision of outstanding flight test programme.
All day visit to industrial firm.

Week 37.
Operational requirements of Fighter Command, by Lecturer from Fighter Command.
Operational requirements of Bomber Command, by Lecturer from Bomber Command.
Operational requirements of Transport Command, by Lecturer from Transport Command.
Revision exercises as required.

Week 38.
Revision lectures and tutorial classes.
Revision exercises as required.

Week 39.
End of course examinations. (Four three-hour papers).
Revision exercises as required.

Weeks 40 & 41.

These two weeks will be devoted to revision and completion of outstanding test work. Revision lectures and discussions will be arranged as and when required. In addition, further external lecturers will be invited to give talks on subjects of interest. The Mc Kenna Trophy will be presented at a dinner to be arranged in the final week.

Bristol Beaufighter and Bill Tacon

The Beaufighter appeared in various marks during its career. The prototype first flew on 17th July 1939 having been a development from the Bristol Beaufort, torpedo bomber. The prototype was powered by the Bristol Hercules MkI-IS engine. The RAF set out a requirement for a long-range heavy fighter. The first operational aircraft MkII fitted with Rolls Royce Merlin XX engines, entered service on 2nd September 1940 in time to take its place in the Battle of Britain with Fighter Command.

The Beaufighter became an extremely capable night fighter when fitted with radar. The Beaufighter went on to serve in Bomber Command, but it was with Coastal Command that it came into its own. Fitted with a range of different armament, it was used for convoy protection, anti-submarine patrols and low-level shipping strikes. In mid-1942 the Beaufighter entered service in the Far East where it was used extensively in a ground attack role in the inhospitable conditions of the jungle covered terrain. It was here that it earned its name of "Whispering Death" due to the fact it was unusually quiet on its approach. The RAAF also used the Beaufighter in large numbers and many were built in Australia. Post war surplus aircraft were sold off to several air forces throughout the world.

The general specification for the Beaufighter,
Crew, 2.
Length, 41ft 7in.
Wingspan, 57ft 10in.
Height, 15ft 10in.
Wing area, 503sqft.
Weight, (empty), 15,592lb Max take-off weight 25,400lb.
Fuel capacity, 550gal up to 682gal with additional internal and external tanks.
Power plant, 2x Bristol Hercules XVII or Hercules XVIII 14 cylinder air-cooled, sleeve valve radial engines.
Propellors, 3-bladed constant speed.
Performance.
Maximum speed, 320mph at 10,000ft.
Range, 1,750miles.
Service ceiling 19,000ft.
Rate of climb, 1,600ft/min.
Armament.
Guns, 4x20mm Hispano MkII Cannon in nose.
6x.303 Browning machine guns in wings, 4 starboard and 2 port, these could be replaced by additional fuel tanks.
1x.303 Vickers Type K gas operated machine gun or Browning machine gun in Observer's cupola.
Rockets, 8x30lb RP3 rocket projectiles.
Bombs, 2x250lb bombs, of various types or 1x18inch torpedo or 1x MK13 torpedo.
The armament varied on the operational requirement for the aircraft, with removals or replacement when required.

Bill Tacon

Wing Commander E W "Bill" Tacon, DSO, DFC and Bar, AFC, and Bar. One of the most decorated pilots in Coastal Command, Bill Tacon had a remarkable career in the RAF. Bill was born on 16th December 1917 at Napier, North Island New Zealand into a farming family. He joined the RNZAF in 1938 and under a scheme where-by New Zealand supplied six trained pilots per year he transferred to the RAF in 1939. Initially flying Avro Ansons then Lockheed Hudsons he was serving with 233 Squadron at the outbreak of war. The first year and a half of his war was spent bombing airfields and on anti-submarine and shipping duties such as escorting Royal Navy vessels during the ill-fated Norway campaign. He was awarded his first DFC in May 1940 and completed his first tour of operations in January 1941. After various training postings in the UK, he was sent to Nova Scotia, Canada. Before leaving the UK, he was awarded the AFC.

Following a return to New Zealand he was then posted to Fiji where he commanded 4 Squadron where he earned a bar to his AFC. Bill returned to the UK and joined 236 Squadron in May 1944. It was for leading the Beaufighter Wing in August 1944 as part of Operation Cork that Bill Tacon was awarded his DSO. In 1946 he resigned his short service commission and took up a permanent commission and was appointed O/C Kings Flight. For his work with the Kings flight, he was made a Member of the Royal Victorian Order in 1947. There followed several overseas postings before his return to the UK in 1963. On his retirement from the RAF in 1970, with the rank of Air Commodore, he returned to New Zealand. He died on the 9th of September 2003 aged 85.